SUCCESS STARTS FROM THE MIND

You Are What You Feed Your Brain

Allen King

Table of Contents

PART 1

Chapter 1:

There's No Time for Regrets

Regret. Guilt. Shame.

These are three of the darkest emotions any human will ever experience. We all feel these things at different points in our lives, especially after making a "bad" decision. There are certain situations some of us would rewind (or delete) if we could. The reality is, however, there is an infinite number of reasons we should never regret any of the decisions we make in our lives.

Here are 7 of them:

Every decision allows you to take credit for creating your own life.

Decisions are not always the result of thoughtful contemplation. Some of them are made on impulse alone. Regardless of the decision, when you made it, it was something you wanted, or you would not have done it (unless someone was pointing a gun at your head).

Be willing to own the decisions you make. Be accountable for them. Take responsibility and accept them.

By making any decision involving your heart, you have the chance to create more love in the world by spreading yours.

Your love is a gift.

Once you decide to love, do it without reservation. By fully giving of yourself, you expand your ability to express and receive love. You have added to the goodness of our universe by revealing your heart to it.

By experiencing the disappointment that might come with a decision's outcome, you can propel yourself to a new level of emotional evolution.

You aren't doing yourself any favors when you try to save yourself from disappointment. Disappointment provides you with an opportunity to redefine your experiences in life. By refining your reframing skills, you increase your resilience.

"Bad" decisions are your opportunity to master the art of self-forgiveness.

When you make a "bad" decision, *you* are the person who is usually the hardest on yourself. Before you can accept the consequences of your decision and move on, you must forgive yourself. You won't always make perfect choices in your life. Acknowledge the beauty in your human imperfection, then move forward and on.

Because of the occasional misstep, you enable yourself to live a Technicolor life.

Anger. Joy. Sadness.

These emotions add pigment to your life. Without these things, you would feel soulless. Your life would be black and white.

Make your decisions with gusto. Breathe with fire. You are here to live in color.

Your ability to make a decision is an opportunity to exercise the freedom that is your birthright.

How would you feel if you had no say in those decisions concerning your life? Would you feel powerless? Restricted? Suffocated?

Now, focus on what it feels like to make the decisions you want to make. What do you feel? Freedom? Liberty? Independence?

What feelings do you *want* to feel?

Freedom. Liberty. Independence.

As luck would have it, the freedom you want is yours. Be thankful for it in every decision you make, "good" or "bad."

When you decide to result in ugly aftermath, you refine what you *do* want in your life.

It's often impossible to know what you want until you experience what you don't want. With every decision, you will experience consequences. Use those outcomes as a jumping-off point to something different (and better) in your future.

Chapter 2:

10 Habits of Taylor Swift

Well-versed pop star isn't the only description for the "American Sweetheart" Taylor Swift- She's a woman with many talents and abilities. As a world-famous singer-songwriter, accomplished businesswoman, and fitness guru, Swift has risen to become one of the world's most renowned celebrities.

She signed her first record deal at the age of 15, has been nominated for over 500 awards, has won 324, and has sold over 50 million albums. Such success did not simply land to her automatically. As per the new Netflix documentary Miss Americana, Swift's growth is a journey of countless disappointing and challenging life and career lessons.

Here are 10 habits of Taylor Swift that can enrich your life and career path.

1. Certainty

Getting to where you want to be in life credits a clear vision. With a sense of clarity, you can pave the way to reach that destination.

Since the day she started her career in music, Taylor Swift has been clear on what she wanted. From the very young age she has served to steer her decision making, and enjoyed every bit of it.

2. Focus on the Brighter Side

Taylor Swift has had a share of public scandals, tabloids exploitation, and people who aimed at tarnishing her name with controversy. It is irrelevant whether they are justified or not, she continues to produce and thrive in her positive space. Just like Taylor Swift, develop an urge to always working past the ruins while strengthening your optimistic moods.

3. You Have No Control Over What Happens

The incident at 2009 VMAs with Kanye West fuelled Swift's desire to prove that her talent is undeniable. You'll learn from the Concert's footage performing her most critically acclaimed song, "All Too Well", that she's was not up to changing what people would eventually say about her but was only concerned with respecting her work ethic. Make your response to criticism a reflection of respect for your hustle!

4. Credit Your Success to Having a Niche

In the entertainment business, and with successful people like Taylor Swift, each one has their unique niche/speciality that sets them apart from everyone else. Major deeply on what makes you unique and what brought you there as your storyline is only for you to tell.

5. Courage Is the Secret to Longevity

Taylor went from being a trial for sexual assault, which she won the case, to her mother ailing from breast cancer and brain tumour to all the publicized stunts she had been through. Despite the challenges, she managed to produce indisputably remarkable projects. Just like Taylor, your confidence, resilience, brilliance, work ethic, and steadfast trust in your process will definitely garner appreciation and respect.

6. Own Your Power

Taylor Swift not only has power, but she also owns it. Following Scooter Braun and Scott Borchetta incident, Taylor was not scared to jeopardize her image or face the consequences of speaking up against something she honestly believed was unfair.

There are always risks to speaking out, but sitting silence may be far riskier. In some circumstances, being silent may endanger your opportunity to manage a project or receive a promotion or increase.

7. Develop Your Support System

Nurture your relationships if you'd like to gain more influence. Even though you are not on the same scale as Taylor Swift, maintained friendships influences your world. Listen to them if you want them to listen to you.

8. Follow Your Heroes

Taylor Swift started her profession at a young age. Her childhood was fraught with difficulties but had motivation from her idols, whom she followed their advice. If you adore someone who influences your life path, emulating two or three things from them pays off.

9. Be Influential

Taylor's success in the music industry has been her driving force in influencing other people. You don't have to have her numbers to be impactful. When you devote your time and energy to becoming productive, influential stats and metrics will follow you.

10. Maintain a Healthy Lifestyle

Being a celebrity doesn't mean that Swift's healthy lifestyle is about trendy diets and strange eating habits that dominates the entire Hollywood culture. According to PopSugar, Swift eats salads, nutritious sandwiches, yoghurt and hit the gym regularly during the week.

Conclusion

You don't have to be Taylor Swift, but you can learn from her. Increase your influence, cultivate your network, develop credibility, wield your authority, focus on positivity, resilience is vital, and feel free to stand your ground as you work on your uniqueness.

Chapter 3:

8 Steps To Develop Beliefs That Will Drive you To Success

'Success' is a broad term. There is no universal definition of success, it varies from person to person considering their overall circumstances. We can all more or less agree that confidence plays a key role in it, and confidence comes from belief.

Even our most minute decisions and choices in life are a result of believing in some specific outcome that we have not observed yet.

However, merely believing in an ultimate success will not bring fortune knocking at your door. But, it certainly can get you started—take tiny steps that might lead you towards your goal. Now, since we agree that having faith can move you towards success, let's look at some ways to rewire your brain into adopting productive beliefs.

Here are 8 Steps to Develop Beliefs That Will Drive You To Success:

1. Come Up With A Goal

Before you start, you need to decide what you want to achieve first. Keep in mind that you don't have to come up with something very specific right away because your expectations and decisions might change over time. Just outline a crude sense of what 'Achievement' and 'Success' mean to you in the present moment.

Begin here. Begin now. Work towards getting there.

2. Put Your Imagination Into Top Gear

"Logic will take you from A to B. Imagination will take you everywhere", said Albert Einstein.

Imagination is really important in any scenario whatsoever. It is what makes us humans different from animals. It is what gives us a reason to move forward—it gives us hope. And from that hope, we develop the will to do things we have never done before.

After going through the first step of determining your goal, you must now imagine yourself being successful in the near future. You have to literally picture yourself in the future, enjoying your essence of fulfilment as vividly as you can. This way, your ultimate success will appear a lot closer and realistic.

3. Write Notes To Yourself

Writing down your thoughts on paper is an effective way to get those thoughts stuck in your head for a long time. This is why children are encouraged to write down what is written in the books instead of memorizing them just by reading. You have to write short, simple, motivating notes to yourself that will encourage you to take actions towards your success. It doesn't matter whether you write in a notebook, or on your phone or wherever—just write it. On top of that, occasionally read what you've written and thus, you will remain charged with motivation at all times.

4. Make Reading A Habit

There are countless books written by successful people just so that they can share the struggle and experience behind their greatest achievements. In such an abundance of manuscripts, you may easily find books that portray narratives similar to your life and circumstances. Get reading and expand your knowledge. You'll get never-thought-before ideas that will guide you through your path to success. Reading such books will tremendously strengthen your faith in yourself, and in your success. Read what other successful people believed in—what drove them. You might even find newer beliefs to hold on to. No wonder why books are called 'Man's best friend'.

5. Talk To People Who Motivates You

Before taking this step, you have to be very careful about who you talk to. Basically, you have to speak out your goals and ambitions in life to someone who will be extremely supportive of you. Just talk to them about what you want, share your beliefs and they will motivate you from time to time towards success. They will act as powerful reminders.

Being social beings, no human can ever reject the gist of motivation coming from another human being—especially when that is someone whom you can rely on comfortably. Humans have been the sole supporter of each other since eternity.

6. Make A Mantra

Self-affirming one-liners like 'I can do it', 'Nothing can stop me', 'Success is mine' etc. will establish a sense of firm confidence in your subconscious mind. Experts have been speculative about the power of our subconscious mind for long. The extent of what it can do is still beyond our grasp. But nonetheless, reciting subtle mantras isn't a difficult task. Do it a couple of times every day and it will remain in your mind for ages, without you giving any conscious thought to it. Such subconscious affirmations may light you up in the right moment and show you the path to success when you least expect it.

7. Reward Yourself From Time To Time

Sometimes, your goals might be too far-fetched and as a result, you'll find it harder to believe in something so improbable right now. In a situation like this, what you can do is make short term objectives that ultimately lead to your main goal and for each of those objectives achieved, treat yourself with a reward of any sort—absolutely anything that pleases you. This way, your far cry success will become more apparent to you in the present time. Instant rewards like these will also keep you motivated and make you long for more. This will drive you to believe that you are getting there, you are getting closer and closer to success.

8. Having Faith In Yourself

Your faith is in your hands alone. How strongly you believe in what you deserve will motivate you. It will steer the way for self-confidence to fulfill your inner self. You may be extremely good at something but due to the lack of faith in your own capabilities, you never attempted it—how will you ever know that you were good at that? Your faith in yourself and your destined success will materialize before you through these rewards that you reserve for yourself. You absolutely deserve this!

Final Thoughts

That self-confidence and belief and yourself, in your capabilities and strengths will make you work towards your goal. Keep in mind that whatever you believe in is what you live for. At the end of the day, each of us believed in something that made us thrive, made us work and move forward. Some believed in the military, some believed in maths, some believed in thievery—everyone had a belief which gave them a purpose—the purpose of materializing their belief in this world. How strongly you hold onto your belief will decide how successful you will become.

Chapter 4:

Six Habits of The Mega-Rich

There are rich people then there are the mega-rich. The distinction between them is as clear as day. The former are still accumulating their wealth while the latter is beyond that. Their focus is no longer on themselves but humanity. Their view of things is through the prism of business and not employment. Their business enterprises are well established and their level of competition is unmatched. They are at the top of the pyramid and have a clear view of things below. Here are six habits of the mega-rich:

1. <u>They Have a Diversified Investment Portfolio</u>

The mega-rich are ardent followers of the saying "do not put all your eggs in one basket." They have stakes in every type of business across many world economies beginning with their country. Their patriotism makes them not leave out their countries when they do business.

With diversified risk across various sectors of the economy, they can remain afloat even during tough economic times. Their companies and businesses also yield high returns because of proper management and their diversification.

2. <u>They Are Generous</u>

The mega-rich people are generous to a fault. They run foundations and non-governmental organizations in their name with a cause to help humanity. It indicates their generosity and desire to help the most vulnerable and needy in society. Generosity is a hard trait to trace these days and it distinguishes the mega-rich from kind people. The generosity of mega-rich people seeks to help the needy permanently by showing them how to fish instead of giving them fish. Such an act liberates families from poverty and promises a brighter future to the younger generation.

3. They Are Neither Petty Nor Trivial

Pettiness is not the character of mega-rich people. They do not have time for small squabbles and fights. Instead, they use their energy in pursuit of more productive goals. Their minds always think of their next big move and ways to improve their businesses. They do not have time to engage in non-issues.

Mega-rich investors do not undertake trivial investments. Their businesses are major leaving people marveling at its grandiose. Jeff Benzos took a trip to space and the world was amazed. The impact the ilk of Benzos has in the world economy is unmatched; securities exchanges and global trade shakes whenever such people make a business move.

4. They Have A Clean Public Image

The mega-rich people manage to maintain a scandalous-free public image. This is crucial for their success. When was the last time you came across a character-damaging story of a wealthy person? It is difficult to recall. Perception tends to stick in the minds of people more than reality. This makes it important for them to guard their reputation with their life.

If you are on the path of joining the exclusive club of the mega-rich, begin cleaning up your reputation if it is a mess. Build a new public image that will portray you as a better person to the world. Mega-rich people intimidate by their angel-like reputations and immense influence on their social status.

5. They Have Great Character

A man's character precedes his reputation. Every wealthy person upgrades his/hers. The mega-rich treasure character too much because they are unable to buy it at any price. It is invaluable. Characterlessness is a type of poverty only curable the hard way. There is no shortcut to it except tireless and intentional channeling of your efforts to strengthen it.

A great character is an asset envied by the great and mighty because most of them fall short of it. There are untold stories of the efforts mega-rich people put to build their character. This has formed part of their routine and life habit.

6. They Champion Global Causes

Mega-rich people are champions of social justice and world causes like climate change and global warming. They give their contribution towards global causes without any self-interest. They are at the forefront offering support in whatever capacity.

They invest in these worthy causes because of the duty of corporate social responsibility they owe the world. It is not a debt they pay but an act they do gladly because they have the best interest of the world at heart.

These six habits of the mega-rich have formed their lifestyle. Walk in their footsteps if you want to become like them. You will command respect from everybody. Your business moves shall determine world market trends and you shall set the pace in every sector of the economy.

Chapter 5:

6 Steps To Focus On Growth

Growth is a lifelong process. We grow every moment from the day we are born until our eventual death. And the amazing thing about growth is that there is no real limit to it.

Now, what exactly is growth? Well, growing is the process of changing from one state to another and usually, it has to be positive; constructive; better-than-before. Although growth occurs equally towards all directions in the early years of our life, the rate of growth becomes more and more narrowed down to only a few particular aspects of our life as we become old. We become more distinctified as individuals, and due to our individuality, not everyone of us can possibly grow in all directions. With our individual personality, experiences, characteristics, our areas of growth become unique to us. Consequently, our chances of becoming successful in life corresponds to how we identify our areas of growth and beam them on to our activities with precision. Let us explore some ways to identify our key areas of growth and utilize them for the better of our life.

1. Identify Where You Can Grow

For a human being, growth is relative. One person cannot grow in every possible way because that's how humans are—we simply cannot do every thing at once. One person may grow in one way while another may grow in a completely different way. Areas of growth can be so unlike that one's positive growth might even seem like negative growth to another person's perspective. So, it is essential that we identify the prime areas where we need to grow. This can be done through taking surveys, asking people or critically analyzing oneself. Find out what lackings do you have as a human being, find out what others think that you lack as a human being. Do different things and note down where you are weak but you have to do it anyway. Then, make a list of those areas where you need growing and move on to the next step.

2. Accept That You Need To Grow In Certain Areas

After carefully identifying your lackings, accept these in your conscious and subconscious mind. Repeatedly admit to yourself and others that you lack so and so qualities where you wish to grow with time.

Never feel ashamed of your shortcomings. Embrace them comfortably because you cannot trully change yourself without accepting that you need to change. Growth is a dynamic change that drags you way out of your comfort zone and pushes you into the wild. And to start on this endeavor for growth, you need to have courage. Growth is a choice that requires acceptance and humility.

3. Remind Yourself of Your Shortcomings

You can either write it down and stick it on your fridge or just talk about it in front of people you've just met—this way, you'll constantly keep reminding yourself that you have to grow out of your lackings. And this remembrance will tell you to try—try improving little by little. Try growing.

It is important to remain consciously aware of these at all times because you never know when you might have to face what. All the little and big things you encounter every day are all opportunities of growth. This takes us to the fourth step:

4. Face Your Problems

Whatever you encounter, in any moment or place in your life is an opportunity created: an opportunity for learning. A very old adage goes: "the more we learn, the more we grow". So, if you don't face your problems and run away from them, then you are just losing the opportunity to learn from it, and thus, losing the opportunity of growing from it. Therefore, facing whatever life throws at you also has an important implication on your overall growth. Try to make yourself useful against all odds. Even if you fail at it, you will grow anyway.

5. Cross The Boundary

So, by now you have successfully identified your areas of growth, you have accepted them, you constantly try to remind yourself of them and you face everything that comes up, head on—never running away. You are already making progress. Now comes the step where you push yourself beyond your current status. You go out of what you are already facing and make yourself appear before even more unsettling circumstances.

This is a very difficult process, but if you grow out of here, nothing can stop you ever. And only a few people successfully make it through. You create your own problems, no one might support you and yet still, you try to push forward, make yourself overcome new heights of difficulties and grow like the tallest tree in the forest. You stand out of the crowd. This can only be done in one or two subjects in a lifetime. So make sure that you know where you want to grow. Where you want to invest that much effort, and time, and dedication. Then, give everything to it. Growth is a life's journey.

6. Embrace Your Growth

After you have crossed the boundary, there is no turning back. You have achieved new heights in your life, beyond what you thought you could have ever done. The area—the subject in which you tried to develop yourself, you have made yourself uniquely specialized in that particular area. You have outgrown the others in that field. It is time for you to make yourself habituated with that and embrace it gracefully. The wisdom you've accumulated through growth is invaluable—it has its roots deeply penetrated into your life. The journey that you've gone through while pursuing your growth will now define you. It is who you are.

As I've mentioned in the first line, "growth is a lifelong process". Growth is not a walk in the park, It is you tracking through rough terrains—steep heights and unexplored depths for an entire lifetime. Follow these simple yet difficult steps; grow into the tallest tree and your life will shine upon you like the graceful summer sun.

Chapter 6:

4 Ways Geniuses Come Up With Great Ideas

Following are thumbnail descriptions of strategies common to the thinking styles of creative geniuses in science, art, and industry throughout history.

1. **Geniuses Look at Problems in Many Different Ways**

Genius often comes from finding a new perspective that no one else has taken. Leonardo da Vinci believed that to gain knowledge about the form of problems, you begin by learning how to restructure them in many different ways. He felt the first way he looked at a problem was too biased toward his usual way of seeing things. He would restructure his problem by looking at it from one perspective and move to another view and still another. With each move, his understanding would deepen, and he would begin to understand the essence of the problem. Einstein's theory of relativity is, in essence, a description of the interaction between different perspectives. Freud's analytical methods were designed to find details that did not fit with traditional perspectives to find a completely new point of view.

In order to creatively solve a problem, the thinker must abandon the initial approach that stems from past experience and re-conceptualize the problem. By not settling with one perspective, geniuses do not merely solve existing problems, like inventing an environmentally friendly fuel. They identify new ones. It does not take a genius to analyze dreams; it required Freud to ask in the first place what meaning dreams carry from our psyche.

2. Geniuses Make Their Thoughts Visible

The explosion of creativity in the Renaissance was intimately tied to the recording and conveying of a vast knowledge in a parallel language, a language of drawings, graphs, and diagrams — as, for instance, in the renowned diagrams of DaVinci and Galileo. Galileo revolutionized science by making his thought visible with charts, maps, and drawings, while his contemporaries used conventional mathematical and verbal approaches.

Once geniuses obtain a certain minimal verbal facility, they seem to develop a skill in visual and spatial abilities, which gives them the flexibility to display information in different ways. When Einstein had thought through a problem, he always found it necessary to formulate his subject in as many different ways as possible, including diagrammatically. He had a very visual mind. He thought in terms of visual and spatial forms rather than thinking along purely mathematical or verbal lines of reasoning. In fact, he believed that words and numbers, as they are written or spoken, did not play a significant role in his thinking process.

3. Geniuses Produce

A distinguishing characteristic of genius is immense productivity. Thomas Edison held 1,093 patents, still the record. He guaranteed productivity by giving himself and his assistants' idea quotas. His own personal quota was one minor invention every ten days and a major innovation every six months. Bach wrote a cantata every week, even when he was sick or exhausted. Mozart produced more than six hundred pieces of music. Einstein is best known for his paper on relativity, but he published 248 other papers. T. S. Elliot's numerous drafts of "The Waste Land" constitute a jumble of good and bad passages that eventually was turned into a masterpiece. In a study of 2,036 scientists throughout history, Dean Kean Simonton of the University of California, Davis found that the most respected produced great works and more "bad" ones. Out of their massive quantity of work came quality. Geniuses produce. Period.

4. Geniuses Make Novel Combinations

Dean Keith Simonton, in his 1989 book Scientific Genius suggests that geniuses are geniuses because they form more novel combinations than the merely talented. His theory has etymology behind it: cogito — "I think — originally connoted "shake together": intelligent the root of "intelligence" means to "select among." This is a clear early intuition about the utility of permitting ideas and thoughts to randomly combine with each other and the utility of selecting from the many the few to retain. Like the highly playful child with a pailful of Legos, a genius constantly combines and recombines ideas, images, and thoughts into different combinations in their conscious and subconscious minds. Consider Einstein's equation, $E=mc2$. Einstein did not invent the concepts of energy, mass, or speed of light. Instead, by combining these concepts in a novel way, he could look at the same world as everyone else and see something different. The laws of heredity on which the modern science of genetics is based are the results of Gregor Mendel, who combined mathematics and biology to create new science.

Chapter 7:

The Power of Imperfect Starts

When you have a goal — starting a business or eating healthier, or traveling the world — it's easy to look at someone who is already doing it and then try to reverse engineer their strategy. In some cases, this is useful. Learning from the experiences of successful people is a great way to accelerate your learning curve.

But it's equally important to remember that the systems, habits, and strategies that successful people are using today are probably not the same ones they were using when they began their journey. What is optimal for them right now isn't necessarily needed for you to get started. There is a difference between the two.

Let me explain.

What is Optimal vs. What is Needed

Learning from others is great, and I do it all the time myself.

But comparing your current situation to someone already successful can often make you feel like you lack the required resources to get started at all. If you look at their optimal setup, it can be really easy to convince yourself that you need to buy new things or learn new skills or meet new people before you can even take the first step toward your goals.

And usually, that's not true. Here are two examples.

Starting a business. When you're an entrepreneur, it's so easy to get obsessed with optimal. This is especially true at the start. I can remember being convinced that my first website would not succeed without a great logo. After all, every popular website I looked at had a professional logo. I've since learned my lesson. Now my "logo" is just my name, and this is the most popular website I've built.

Eating healthy. Maybe the optimal diet would involve buying beef that is only grass-fed or vegetables that are only organic, or some other super-healthy food strategy. But if you're just trying to make strides in the right direction, why get bogged down in the details? Start small and simply buy another vegetable this week — whether it's organic or not. There will be plenty of time for optimization later.

Avoiding by Optimizing

Claiming that you need to "learn more" or "get all of your ducks in a row" can often be a crutch that prevents you from moving forward on the stuff that matters.

- You can complain that your golf game is suffering because you need new clubs, but the truth is you probably just need two years of practice.

- You can point out how your business mentor is successful because they use XYZ software, but they probably got started without it.

Obsessing about the ultimate strategy, diet, or golf club can be a clever way to prevent yourself from doing hard work.

An imperfect start can always be improved, but obsessing over a perfect plan will never take you anywhere on its own.

Chapter 8:

The Daily Routine Experts for Peak Productivity

What is the one thing we want to get done for a successful life? That is an effective daily routine to go through the day, every day. History is presented as an example that every high achiever has had a good routine for their day. Some simple changes in our life can change the outcome drastically. We have to take the experts' advice for a good lifestyle. We have to choose everything, from color to college, ourselves. But an expert's advice gives us confidence in our choice.

You have to set the bar high so that you get your product at the end of the day. Experts got their peak productivity by shaping their routine in such a way that it satisfies them. The productivity expert Tim Ferriss gave us a piece of simple yet effective advice for such an outcome. He taught us the importance of controlling oneself and how essential it is to provide yourself with a non-reactive practice. When you know how to control yourself, life gets more manageable, as it gives you the power to prevent many things. It reduces stress which gets your productivity out.

Another productive expert of ours, Cal Newport, gives us his share of information. He is always advising people to push themselves to their limits. He got successful by giving his deep work more priority than other work. He is managing multitasks at the same time while being a husband and a father. He is a true example of a good routine that leads to positive productivity. It would help if you decided what matters to you the most and need to focus on that. Get your priorities straight and work toward those goals. Construct your goals and have a clear idea of what your next step will be. It will result in increasing your confidence.

Now, the questions linger that how to start your day? Early is the answer. Early to bed and early to rising has been the motto of productive people. As Dan Ariely said, there is a must 3 hours in our day when our productivity is at its peak. A morning person hit more products, as it's said that sunrise is when you get active. Mostly from 8 o'clock to 10 o'clock. It's said that morning is the time when our minds work the sharpest. It provides you alertness and good memory ability. It is also called the "protected time." We get a new sense to think from, and then we get a sound vision of our steps and ideas to a routine of peak productivity.

Charles Duhigg is a known news reporter, works for the New York Times. He tells us to stop procrastinating and visualizing our next step in life. Not only does it give you confidence, but it also gives you a satisfactory feeling. You get an idea of the result, and you tend to do things more that way. This way, you get habitual of thinking about your next step beforehand. Habits are gradually formed. They are difficult to change but easy to assemble. A single practice can bring various elements from it. Those elements can help you learn the routine of an expert.

You will eventually fall into place. No one can change themselves in one day. Hard work is the key to any outcome. Productivity is the result of many factors but, an excellent daily routine is an integral part of it which we all need to follow. Once you fall into working constantly, you won't notice how productive you have become. It becomes a habit. There might be tough decisions along the way, which is typical for an average life. We need to focus on what's in front of us and start with giving attention to one single task on top of your priority list. That way, you can achieve more in less time. These are some factors and advice to start a daily routine for reaching the peak of productivity with the help of some great products.

7 Habits To Change Your Life

Consistently, habit drives you to do what you do—regardless of whether it's a matter of considerations or conduct that happens naturally. Whatever that is, imagine a scenario where you could saddle the power of your habits to improve things. Envision a day to day existence where you have a habit for finishing projects, eating admirably, staying in contact with loved ones, and working to your fullest potential. At the point when you have an establishment of beneficial routines, you're setting yourself up for a full, sound, and effective life.

Here are 7 habits that Can change your entire life.

1. Pinpoint and Focus Entirely on Your Key stone Routine.

Charles Duhigg, in his power book stipulates the essence of recognizing your Keystone Habit—the habit you distinguish as the main thing you can change about your life. To discover what that is for you, ask yourself, what continually worries you? Is it something you would that you like to stop, or something you would do and prefer not to begin? The cornerstone habit is distinctive for everybody, and it might take a couple of meetings of profound thought to pinpoint precisely what that habit is.

Whichever propensity you're chipping away at, pick each in turn. More than each in turn will be overpowering and will improve your probability of neglecting to improve any habits. Be that as it may, don't really accept that you can just change one thing about yourself; it's really the inverse. Dealing with this one Keystone Habit can have a positive gradually expanding influence into the remainder of your life also.

2. Recognize Your Present Daily Practice a nd the Reward You Get From It.

Suppose you need to fabricate a habit for getting to the workplace a half hour early every day. You need to do this since you figured the extra peaceful time in the morning hours will assist you with being more gainful, and that profitability will be compensated by an expanded feeling of occupation fulfilment, and a generally speaking better workplace. As of now, you get to the workplace simply on schedule. Your present routine is to take off from your home in a hurry, at the specific time you've determined that (without traffic or episode) will get you to chip away at time. Your award is investing some additional energy at your home in the first part of the day, spending an additional half hour dozing or "charging your batteries" for the day ahead.

3. Take the Challenges Into Consideration.

Challenges are regularly prompts that push you to fall once more into old habits. In the case of having to get to work earlier, your challenges may lie in your rest designs the prior night, or in organizing plans with a partner. These difficulties won't mysteriously vanish so you need to consider them. In any case, don't let the presence of challenges, or stress that new difficulties will come up later on, discourage you from setting up your new propensities. In the event that your difficulties incorporate planning with others, make them a piece of your new daily practice, as I'll clarify later. At this moment, basically recognize what the difficulties or obstructions are.

4. Plan and Identifying Your New Routine.

Old habits never vanish; they are basically supplanted with new propensities. In the case of getting to the workplace earlier, the new standard includes going out a half hour sooner. On the off chance that the old habit was remunerated with the possibility that you'll have more energy for the day by remaining in your home longer, the new propensity needs to centre around the possibility that more rest doesn't really mean more energy. All in all, you'll need to address what you think you'll be surrendering by supplanting the old habit.

5. Reinforce a 30 Days Challenge.

By and large, your inability to minister beneficial routines basically comes from not adhering to them. A lot of studies show that habits, when performed day by day, can turn out to be important for your daily schedule in just 21 days. So set a beginning date and dispatch your game plan for a preliminary 30-day time span.

6. Empower Your Energy Through Setbacks

Here and there, it's not simply self-control that runs out. Now and then you are influenced from your ways by life "hindering" new objectives. In the event that something influences you from your test, the best game-plan is to assess the circumstance and perceive how you can get around, finished, or through that deterrent. Notwithstanding, when another propensity is set up, it really turns into our default setting. Assuming your standard habits are sound, unpleasant occasions are less inclined to lose you from your typical schedules. All in all, we're similarly prone to default to solid habits as we are to self-undermining habits, if those sound habits have become a piece of our ordinary daily practice.

7. Account Yourself and for Your Actions P ublicly (Hold Yourself Accountable).

Your encouraging people are the most significant asset you will have at any point. Regardless of whether it's your closest companion, your accomplice or your Facebook posts, being responsible to somebody other than yourself will help you adhere to your objective. Simply remember that "responsible" isn't equivalent to "declaration". Anybody can advise the world they will rise ahead of schedule from here on out. However, on the off chance that that individual has a group of allies behind them, whom they routinely update, they are bound to stay with their new propensity during times when they are building up their new habit and inspiration is coming up short.

Chapter 9:

8 Ways On How To Start

Taking Actions

Have you ever got caught up in situations when you can't bring yourself moving from deciding to doing? As a famous person once said, "Your beliefs become your thoughts; your thoughts become your words; your words become your actions; your actions become your habits; your habits become your values; your values become your destiny."

The first step towards success is by taking action. If you keep on thinking that you have to lose weight, start a business, learn a new language, or get another degree, you will end up nowhere without executing these thoughts into actions.

Here are 8 Ways To Start Moving The Needle In Your Life:

1. Decide that you want to get out of your comfort zone

The fear that we have that doesn't allow us to take action is that we might have to sacrifice our comfort zone in the process. And trust me, a lot of people aren't willing to do that. But if you don't step out of your comfort zone, how will you determine your true potential? You don't need the motivation to start taking action, and you just have to gather your willpower, stop with the excuses and procrastination, and get moving!

2. Don't indulge in the habit of Hesitatation

Have you had a great idea but then decide 10 minutes later that it was stupid. Ever wondered why that was? The answer is quite simple and straightforward; hesitation. We dwell on hesitation for too long. This makes it very difficult for us to get started on something. Thinking will only lead us to more and more thinking, which will lead us to a loop of continual thoughts, and our actions will get dominated by them. And then the regret that follows us is usually, "Why didn't we start earlier?" David Joseph Schwartz once said, "To fight fear, act. To increase fear – wait, put off, postpone."

3. Stop waiting for the perfect time:

There's a Chinese proverb that says, "The best time to plant a tree was 20 years ago. The second-best time is now." It means that there is no such thing as perfect timing. The minute we start to take action, the time becomes perfect. If we wait till everything gets in order or becomes exemplary, then we will be waiting forever. The ideal time in your eyes was last year, but the second-best time is right here and right now. It's never too late to start with your goals, dreams, and passions. All we have in our hands is the present time and what counts is how efficiently we spend this time. We must take action now and make adjustments along the way if we feel like it.

4. Don't pause and wait:

Have you ever found yourself thinking that, hey, it's a good day to wander around the city, but found yourself sitting and wasting time watching TV? Or you thought of doing your assignment but got caught up in a more hopeless task? Or you thought of presenting a new idea to your boss but got shied away? All of these thoughts, no matter how positive they were, stand nowhere unless you implement them. So stop being a talker and start being a doer. A doer is someone who immediately moves forward with his ideas. When we pause and look around, we will find ourselves making excuses and allow doubts to creep through into our minds. "The most difficult thing is the decision to act; the rest is merely tenacity." - Amelia Earhart.

5. Stop Over-thinking:

There's always an endless loop of overthinking that we can't get over with no matter how hard we try. From imagining the worst-case scenarios of even the best situations to getting anxious and depressed whenever any minor inconvenience happens, our mind tricks us into thinking that we can never get the best of both worlds (HM fans, I gotcha!) When we overthink stuff, we tend to get paralysis of analysis. We start to analyze every situation and obsess over how things aren't perfect, or the conditions aren't going our way. We question the amount of time that we have to commit and make endless excuses and reasons not to move forward with whatever we want to do.

6. Take continuous action:

The first step is the hardest step that we have to take. But once you get started, make sure that you fully commit yourself to your goal. Take continuous actions and keep up with your momentum by doing something related to your plan every day. Even if you are scheduling only 15-20 minutes of your life completing a small task, it will eventually add up into the more remarkable things. Moreover, it will help you build confidence by seeing your achievements. "It does not matter how slowly you go as long as you do not stop." - Confucius.

7. Overcome your fears:

We often succumb to our fears before even taking a step. The fear of failure, of not being good enough, of not doing enough, is the most common among them. Our mind tricks us into thinking that we might end up failing sooner or later. This prevents us from taking the first step and implementing our thoughts into actions. For example, suppose you're a professional speaker at a public speaking event. You have gained loads of experience, and you have no problem speaking to the lobby. But you do feel yourself getting nervous when you have to wait around for your turn. However, once you get started, all that fear and anxiety disappear. If you face similar situations in life, start being a doer, take action towards it and see how it will boost your confidence.

8. Eliminate any distractions:

We live in a world where distractions and procrastination have become more important than productivity. Have you ever found yourself thinking that you will take the online lecture for the subject you have been struggling with but ended up checking your social media accounts or watching irrelevant videos on YouTube? Procrastination is the primary reason we never end up doing what we should keep in our priorities. Instead, we should focus on our tasks, eliminate all the distractions and start with a slow but steady pace towards our goal. A single average idea put into action is far more valuable than those 20 genius ideas saved for another day or another time.

Conclusion:

Achieving your goals and dreams isn't an overnight task but takes years and decades to give you the final fruits. It's a road that will have setbacks, obstacles, lessons, and challenges. But what matters is that we shouldn't give up. We should face all the struggles and not surrender ourselves to our fears and demotivation. Converting your thoughts into actions and then enjoying the journey will equip you to thrive and see your goals become a reality in no time. So take into account what steps you took today. No matter how small they may be, appreciate and celebrate them.

PART 2

Chapter 1:

Visualise Your Success In Life

When you have a clear idea of what you want in life, it becomes easier to achieve somehow. When you visualize yourself doing something, you automatically tend to get the results better. You can imagine your success in your mind before you even reach it so that it gives you a sense of comfort. You get the confidence that you can do whatever you desire. You complete your task more quickly because you have already done it once in your mind before even starting it. It relaxes us so we can interpret the outcome. You dream about your goals and remind yourself almost every day what you genuinely want or need. You become goal-oriented just by imagining your outcomes and results. Your brain tends to provide you with every possible option of opportunity you can have by visualizing. By this, you can take your dreams and desire into the real world and achieve them by knowing the possible outcome already.

Everyone today wants their picture-perfect life. They are derived from working for it, and they even manage to achieve it sometimes. People love the success which they had already estimated to happen one day. They knew they would be successful because they not only worked for it but, they also visualized it in their brains. Everything eventually falls into place once you remind yourself of your goals constantly and sometimes write it into a few words. Writing your goals down helps you immensely. It is the idea of a constant reminder for you. So, now whenever you look on that paper or note, you find yourself recognizing your path towards success. That is one of the ways you could visualize yourself as a successful person in the coming era.

Another way to visualize your success is through private dialogue. One has to talk its way through success. It's a meaningful way to know your heart's content and what it is you are looking for in this whole dilemma. You can then easily interpret your thoughts into words. It becomes easier to tell people what you want. It is an essential factor to choose between something. Weighing your options, analyzing every detail, and you get your answer. It requires planning for every big event ahead and those to come. You ready yourself for such things beforehand so that you will know the result.

Every single goal of yours will count. So, we have to make sure that we give our attention to short-term goals and long-term goals. We have to take in the details, not leaving anything behind in the way or so. We have to make sure that everything we do is considered by ourselves first. Short-term goals are necessary for you to achieve small incomes, giving you a sense of pride. Long-term plans are more time-consuming, and it takes a lot of hard work and patience from a person. Visualizing a long-term goal might be a risk, something as big as a long-term achievement can have loads of different outcomes, and we may get distracted from our goal to become successful in life. But, visualizing does help you work correctly to get to know what will be your next step. You can make schemes in your mind about specific projects and how to work them out. Those scheming will help you in your present and future. So, it is essential to look at every small detail and imagine short-term goals and long-term goals.

Visualizing your success creates creative ideas in your mind. Your mind gets used to imagining things like these, and it automatically processes the whole plan in your mind. You then start to get more ideas and opportunities in life. You just need to close your eyes and imagine whatever you need to in as vivid detail as possible. Almost everything done by you is a result of thoughts of your mind. It is like another person living inside of you, who tells you what to do. It asks you to be alert and move. It also means the result of the possible outcome of a situation. Every action of you is your mind. Every word you speak is your mind talking.

Chapter 2:

Five Habits For A Beautiful Life

A beautiful life means different things to different people. However, there are some things that we can all agree about. It is a happy one. Some of us have chased this kind of life but it has proven elusive to the brink of throwing in the towel. We play a greater role in designing a beautiful life for ourselves than others do in our lives.

Here are five habits for a beautiful life:

1. Live The Moment

This is not a call to carelessness. The focal point is to cherish the present moment. We are often distracted by our past experiences even in times when we ought to celebrate our current wins. The present is beautiful because we can influence it.

A beautiful life is joyous and the envy of those who cannot experience it. Savor the present completely and do not be entangled in the past. The past will withhold you from leveraging the opportunities popping up presently. Every saint has a past and every sinner has a future. You can shape the future by living in the moment and not dwelling in the past.

Worrying about the future is not beneficial. If you can change a situation, why worry? If you cannot also change anything, why worry? It is pointless to take the burden of occurrences that are yet to happen. Enjoy your present successes while you can and lead the beautiful life you have been dreaming of.

2. Plan Wisely

Like everything invaluable, a beautiful life should be planned for. Planning is an integral part of determining whether a beautiful flawless life is achievable or not. It is not an event but a process that requires meticulous attention.

Planning entails extensive allocation of resources to life priorities. You should get your priorities right for things to run smoothly. In planning, your judgment and conscience should be as clear as a cloudless night. Any conflict of interest that could arise will jeopardize the attainment of a beautiful life - the ultimate goal.

We may be forced to make some painful sacrifices along the way and possibly give up short-time pleasures for long-term comfort. It may bring some discomfort but is worth the attainment of a beautiful life. Planning is a heavy price that must be made a routine to anyone aspiring to this magnificent dream.

3. Pursue Your Purpose

Your purpose is the sole reason that keeps you going in life. You should pursue what motivates you to keep chasing your dreams. A beautiful life is one of fulfillment. Your purpose will bring it effortlessly if you remain loyal to it.

Focusing on your purpose can be a daunting task to an undisciplined mind. Many distractions may come up to make you stray or shift goalposts. You need to be disciplined to continue treading in the narrow path of your purpose. Do not lose sight of the antelope (a beautiful life) because of a dashing squirrel (distractions).

Living a life of purpose will satisfy you because you will willfully do what brings you joy; not what circumstances have forced you to. A cheerful way to live each day like it is your last is by finding pleasure in your routine activities and by extension, your purpose. Pursue it boldly!

4.   Cut Your Coat According To Your Cloth

Live within your means and cut on unnecessary costs. Many people struggle to live within a particular social class that they are not able to afford at the moment. In the process of fitting in, they incur unmanageable debt.

A beautiful life does not mean one of luxury. It is stress-free and affordable within your space. It is unimaginable that one will wear himself/herself out to live a lifestyle beyond reach. Societal pressure should not push you to the brink of self-destruction as you try to fit in other people's shoes.

Even as you work towards your goals, do not suffocate yourself to please other people. Accept your financial status and make your budget within it. You will have an authentic and beautiful life.

5.   Share Your Life With Your Loved Ones

We all have our families and loved ones. Our parents, siblings, spouses, and children should share our lives with us. It is beautiful and desirable that we intertwin our social and personal lives. The warmth and love of our families will put a smile on our faces despite any challenges.

Often, our families are the backbone of our emotional support. We retreat to them when we are wounded by the struggles of life and they nurse us back to health. Their presence and contribution to our lives are immeasurable. Family does not necessarily mean you have to be related by blood.

Some people are strong pillars in our lives and have seen us through hard times. Over time, they have become part of our family. We should share our lives with them and treasure each moment. We would be building a beautiful life for ourselves and the upcoming generations.

These are five habits we need to develop for a beautiful life. We only live once and should enjoy our lifetime by all means.

Chapter 3:

5 Ways To Adopt Right Attitude For Success

Being successful is a few elements that require hard work, dedication, and a positive attitude. It requires building your resilience and having a clear idea of your future ahead. Though it might be hard to decide your life forward, a reasonable manner is something that comes naturally to those who are willing to give their all. Adopting a new attitude doesn't always mean to change yourself in a way but, it has more meaning towards changing your mindset to an instinct. That is when you get stressed or overworked is because of an opposing point of view on life.

With success comes a great sense of dealing with things. You become more professional, and you feel the need to achieve more in every aspect. Don't be afraid to be power-hungry. But, it also doesn't mean to be unfair. Try to go for a little more than before, each step ahead. Make your hard work or talent count in every aspect. Make yourself a successful person in a positive manner, so you'll find yourself making the most of yourself. And don't give up on the things you need in life.

1. Generate Pragmatic Impressions

"The first impression is the last impression." It's true that once you've introduced yourself to the person in front of you, there is only a tiny chance that you'll get to introduce yourself again. So, choosing the correct wording while creating an impression is a must. You need to be optimistic about yourself and inform the other person about you in a way that influences them. An impression that leaves an effect on them, so they will willingly meet you again. A person must be kind and helpful towards its inferior and respectful towards their superior. This is one of the main characteristics for a person to be a successful man or woman. And with a negative attitude, the opposite occurs. People are more inclined to work without you. They nearly never consider you to work with them and try to contact you as little as possible. So, a good impression is significant.

2. Be True To Your Words

Choose your wording very carefully, because once said, it can't be taken back. Also, for a successful life, commitment is always an important rule. Be true to what you said to a person. Make them believe that they can trust you comfortably. So, it would be best if you chose your words. Don't commit if you can't perform. False commitment leads to loss of customers and leads to the loss of your impression as a successful worker. Always make sure that you fulfill your commands and promises to your clients and make them satisfied with your performance. It leads to a positive mindset and a dedication to work towards your goal.

3. A Positive Personal Life

Whatever you may be doing in your professional life can impact your personal life too. Creating the right mindset professionally also helps you to keep a positive attitude at home. It allows you to go forward with the proper consultation with your heart. It will make you happier. You'll desire to achieve more in life because you'll be satisfied with your success. It will push to go furthermore. It will drive you towards the passion for desiring more. Hard work and determination will continue to be your support, and you will be content will your heart. By keeping a good attitude, you'll be helping yourself more than helping others.

4. Be Aggressive and Determined

Becoming goal-oriented is one of the main factors evolving success in your life. If you are not determined to do your work, you'll just accept things the way others present you. It will leave you in misery and deeply dissatisfied with yourself. Similarly, you'll tend to do something more your way if you are goal-oriented and not how others want. You'll want to shale everything according to your need, and you become delighted with yourself and the result of your hard work. Always keep a clear view of your next step as it will form you in to your true self. Don't just go with the flow, but try to change it according to your wants and needs.

5. Create Your Master Plan

Indeed, we can't achieve great things with only hard work. We will always need to add a factor or to in our business. But by imagining or strategizing, some plans might be helpful. With hard work and some solid projects, we will get our desired outcome. If not, at least we get something close. And if you chose the wrong option, then the amount of hard work won't matter. You'll never get what you want no matter the hard work. So, always make sure to make plans strategically.

Conclusion

By keeping a positive attitude, you'll not only be helpful to others but to yourself too. Make sure you keep the proper manner—a manner required to be a successful person. Do lots of achievements and try to prove yourself as much as possible. Try keeping a good impact on people around you in everything you do. Have the spirit and courage to achieve great heights. And be sure to make moat of yourself. Consistency is the key.

Chapter 4:

5 Tips to Increase Your Attention Span

If you've ever found it difficult to get through a challenging task at work, studied for an important exam, or spent time on a finicky project, you might have wished you could increase your ability to concentrate.

Concentration refers to the mental effort you direct toward whatever you're working on or learning at the moment. It's sometimes confused with attention span, but attention span refers to the length of time you can concentrate on something.

If that sounds familiar, keep reading to learn more about research-backed methods to help improve your attention span. We'll also go over some conditions that can affect concentration and steps to take if trying to increase concentration on your own just doesn't seem to help.

1. Train Your Brain

Playing certain types of games can help you get better at concentrating. Try:

- sudoku

- crossword puzzles

- chess

- jigsaw puzzles

- word searches or scrambles

- memory games

Results of a 2015 study Trusted Source of 4,715 adults suggest spending 15 minutes a day, five days a week, on brain training activities can greatly impact concentration.

Brain training games can also help you develop your working and short-term memory, as well as your processing and problem-solving skills.

Older adults

The effects of brain training games may be particularly important for older adults since memory and concentration often tend to decline with age.

Research from 2014Trusted Source that looked at 2,832 older adults followed up on participants after ten years. Older adults who completed between 10 and 14 cognitive training sessions saw improved cognition, memory, and processing skills.

After ten years, most study participants reported they could complete daily activities at least as well as they could at the beginning of the trial, if not better.

2. Get Your Game On

Brain games may not be the only type of game that can help improve concentration. Newer research also suggests playing video games could help boost concentration.

A 2018 study looking at 29 people found evidence to suggest an hour of gaming could help improve visual selective attention (VSA). VSA refers to your ability to concentrate on a specific task while ignoring distractions around you.

Its small size limited this study, so these findings aren't conclusive. The study also didn't determine how long this increase in VSA lasted.

Study authors recommend future research continue exploring how video games can help increase brain activity and boost concentration.

3. Improve Sleep

Sleep deprivation can easily disrupt concentration, not to mention other cognitive functions, such as memory and attention.

Occasional sleep deprivation may not cause too many problems for you. But regularly failing to get a good night's sleep can affect your mood and performance at work.

Being too tired can even slow down your reflexes and affect your ability to drive or do other daily tasks.

A demanding schedule, health issues, and other factors sometimes make it difficult to get enough sleep. But it's important to try and get as close to the recommended amount as possible on most nights.

Many experts recommend adults aim for 7 to 8 hours of sleep each night.

4. Make Time For Exercise

Increased concentration is among the many benefits of regular exercise. Exercise benefits everyone. A 2018 study looking at 116 fifth-graders found evidence to suggest daily physical activity could help improve both concentration and attention after just four weeks.

Another Source looking at older adults suggests that just a year of moderate aerobic physical activity can help stop or reverse memory loss that occurs with brain atrophy related to age.

Do what you can

Although aerobic exercise is recommended, doing what you can is better than doing nothing at all. Depending on your fitness and weight goals, you may want to exercise more or less.

But sometimes, it just isn't possible to get the recommended amount of exercise, especially if you live with physical or mental health challenges.

5. Spend Time In Nature

If you want to boost your concentration naturally, try to get outside every day, even for just 15 to 20 minutes. You might take a short walk through a park. Sitting in your garden or backyard can also help. Any natural environment has benefits.

Scientific evidence increasingly supports the positive impact of natural environments. Research from 2014Trusted Source found evidence to suggest including plants in office spaces helped increase concentration and productivity and workplace satisfaction, and air quality.

Try adding a plant or two to your workspace or home for a range of positive benefits. Succulents make great choices for low-maintenance plants if you don't have a green thumb.

Chapter 5:

The Downside of Work-Life Balance

One way to think about work-life balance is with a concept known as The Four Burners Theory. Here's how it was first explained to me:

Imagine that a stove represents your life with four burners on it. Each burner symbolizes one major quadrant of your life.

1. The first burner represents your family.

2. The second burner is your friends.

3. The third burner is your health.

4. The fourth burner is your work.

The Four Burners Theory says that "to be successful, you have to cut off one of your burners. And to be successful, you have to cut off two." **The View of the Four Burners**

My initial reaction to The Four Burners Theory was to search for a way to bypass it. "Can I succeed and keep all four burners running?" I wondered.

Perhaps I could combine two burners. "What if I lumped family and friends into one category?"

Maybe I could combine health and work. "I hear sitting all day is unhealthy. What if I got a standing desk?" Now, I know what you are thinking. Believing that you will be healthy because you bought a standing desk is like believing you are a rebel because you ignored the fasten seatbelt sign on an airplane, but whatever.

Soon I realized I was inventing these workarounds because I didn't want to face the real issue: life is filled with tradeoffs. If you want to excel in your work and your marriage, then your friends and your health may have to suffer. If you want to be healthy and succeed as a parent, then you might be forced to dial back your career ambitions. Of course, you are free to divide your time equally among all four burners, but you have to accept that you will never reach your full potential in any given area.

Essentially, we are forced to choose. Would you rather live a life that is unbalanced but high-performing in a certain area? Or would you rather live a life that is balanced but never maximizes your potential in a given quadrant?

Option 1: Outsource Burners

We outsource small aspects of our lives all the time. We buy fast food, so we don't have to cook. We go to the dry cleaners to save time on laundry. We visit the car repair shop, so we don't have to fix our automobile.

Outsourcing small portions of your life allow you to save time and spend it elsewhere. Can you apply the same idea to one quadrant of your life and free up time to focus on the other three burners?

Work is the best example. For many people, work is the hottest burner on the stove. It is where they spend the most time, and it is the last burner to get turned off. In theory, entrepreneurs and business owners can outsource the work burner. They do it by hiring employees.

The Four Burners Theory reveals a truth everyone must deal with: nobody likes being told they can't have it all, but everyone has constraints on their time and energy. Every choice has a cost.

Which burners have you cut off?

Chapter 6:

Never Give Up

3 Reasons to Carry on Believing in Yourself During Dark Times

We all have black moments. Sometimes these stretch into days, weeks and even months. Both small and huge problems can quickly overwhelm us. There are many reasons.

When we are really down, it may begin to feel like we are living a lifetime of hell. We get caught up in a swirling torrent of negativity. Light and hope fade. Emotionally and psychologically, we become spent. At the extreme, we might even begin to tell ourselves that we will never achieve success, happiness and joy ever again.

Avoiding sinking deeper and deeper into an unpleasant pit of despair can be avoided!

You need to recognize tipping points quickly. It is our cue to stop! Before you go down this rabbit hole, get proper perspective. The sooner the better. Think about it:

1. Stop Focusing Predominantly on Others

Do you still primarily look for external validation? Constantly worrying. For example, what your father wanted you to become? What he thinks of you because you flunked out of university? What he is going to say now when he hears your boss said you are the worst sales performer this month! His views on you facing the horrible prospect of unemployment?

Everyone sees things differently. Actually, accepting we have very little control of what others think, feel and do is helpful. Making paramount what we think, feel and do about our life's direction and quality makes all the different. By doing this we no longer need anyone else's stamp of approval.

When we stop seeking others validation, we start seeking an authentic life. It suddenly becomes uniquely ours. Self-endorsement also feels good. Giving ourselves permission to take charge and chart our own course offers a sense of freedom. We begin to see clearly that at the end of the day, we are the best judges of our lives. It can become well lived on our terms. Let go of the rest.

2. Stop Believing Things Will Not Change

Past regrets aside, recognize you are in the here and now. Without that university degree you are never going to be that doctor your father wanted! However, you do have new options every moment. Seeing new and even creative opportunities during difficulties is the ultimate determinant of your ability to bounce back, turn things around and pursue a brighter future. Short of being fired or dying, there is still time to become the top sales person. It depends if you want it enough.

Think about the different periods, people and situations in your life.

Each of us is living proof of constant change. We certainly can't stop the cycle of change. Our only option is really how we respond to the constant flow. Growth and progress are about making the most of change including obstacles and challenges. Often, we will deny the inevitability of change in an attempt to try avoid confronting our worst fears. We may fail. Again, and yet again. We need to find the courage to go for it irrespective. Committing to the idea that embracing change gives us another opportunity to get better and learn. Current results are temporary and stepping stones.

3. Stop Not Seeing Your Worth

When important people in our lives tell us that we are not good enough, it can be earth shattering. When we tell ourselves, we are not good enough, this is outright dangerous. Especially so if we are astute enough to know that the most significant opinion in our life is our own. Any lack of self-worth limits potential to come out undamaged from dark periods. We can get over the bosses' views that we will never cut it as a high-flying sales guru. But it becomes impossible to lift ourselves up and see the

Chapter 7:

8 Habits That Make People Dislike You

As human beings, we all have a deep innate need to be liked. It's very easy for someone to make a sweeping judgement based on their first impression of you. The vast majority believe that being likable is a matter of natural, inexplicable traits that only belong to a fortunate few; good looks, fierce social media, among others. The reality is that every detail matters; from your interpersonal skills, your last name, your smell, and so on. Generally speaking, certain behaviors make people hold back from liking you. Unless you get such habits done with, it's always easy to fall prey to the unlikeable discrepancy.

Here are 8 habits that makes people dislike you.

1. Self-Indulgence

On the top of the list is a self-centered person. If you are always talking about yourself, greedy, or simply just so full of it, it's not easy to understand why people will find you very annoying. If you are always bragging about your triumphs or lamenting about your problems, be prepared for people to avoid you. If the talk is just about you, and you always, you will be avoided at all costs. Focus on others and their problems instead of your own. Let them share their thoughts and ideas with you equally; that is the basic foundation of a conversation. Don't be full of yourself!

2. Being Too Serious.

People are drawn to enthusiastic individuals. However, because they are often absorbed in their work, enthusiastic people can become too serious or uninterested. This is a turn off as people will find you likable only when you take pride in work while paving way for fun moments too. Which means that you are serious with whatever you are doing but also cherish those socially fun times. This, in turn, demonstrates that the moments you share with others are just as important as your work.

3. Narrow-Mindedness and Rigidity.

When you are open-minded, you are easily likable and approachable. This is in contrast to rigidity and narrow-minded traits. When you are conversing with someone, you must be willing to accept all opinions that differ from yours, even if you don't always agree with them. You may not like what everyone has to say all the time, but it does not imply that you start picking fights and arguing about every small matter. An open-minded person is approachable and so likable. People can talk to you about anything because they know you will not be upset. They will not fear being judged by you because you portray a neutral aura.

If you go into a debate with preconceived views, you are unable to see things from someone else's perspective. It will lead to disputes and arguments. Nobody loves someone who is rigid and judgmental.

4. Dishonesty and Emotional Manipulation

One of the most typical traits of unlikable people is dishonesty. Everyone lies at some point in their lives, but people begin to avoid you when lying becomes a habit. You may lose good friends as a result of this tendency. Dishonest people are frequently manipulative. Instead of confessing their shortcomings, they would tell a lie to avoid an awkward scenario. They can concoct a thousand lies to conceal a single fact. If you engage in the habit of lying, people will quickly see your true colors and you may see your friends dropping like flies.

5. **You Are a Gossip Mogul.**

When people get carried away with gossiping, they make themselves look awful. Wallowing in gossip about other people's actions or misfortunes may end up hurting their feelings if the gossip reaches them. What's more, it's that gossip will always make you look unpleasant and bitter. People will associate you with as the person who goes around spreading rumors and misinformation to others. You may begin to be viewed as untrustworthy in other people's eyes and people will stop telling you things.

6. **A Name-Dropper.**

One of the most vexing hobbies of unlikable people is name-dropping. It is advantageous if you know a few influential and well-known people. Name-dropping in every conversation, on the other hand, will make you obnoxious and unlikable. Name-dropping is a characteristic of insecure persons who are always looking for attention. People will know who you are with without you having to mention it on every occasion. Nobody likes someone who always feels the need to appear superior or more important than others. Sure it'll be interesting to engage in conversations about these people you know, but do it wisely.

7. You Are Constant Phone-Checker.

Checking the phone while having a moment with someone is one of the worst habits of dislikeable people. It is just awful! You should opt out of it.

When you are alone, it is ok to look at your smartphone. However, continuously checking your phone while eating dinner with someone or attending a meeting is impolite. It implies that you are not paying attention to the person who is trying to have this conversation with you. Being addicted or glued to your phone all the time will give the impression that nothing is more important to you than your screen time. You will find that it turns people off and you may not get asked out for a meal again. Don't be so distracted. Pay attention to the person all the time.

8. Sharing Too Much Information, Too Soon.

Chatting up with others necessitates a decent standard of sharing; sharing too much about yourself straight away however, may be inappropriate. Take caution not to share personal concerns or admissions too early. Likable people allow the others to direct them when it is appropriate for them to open up. Oversharing might have an impression that you are self-centered and unconcerned about conversation balance. Consider this: if you dive into the details of your life without first learning about the other person, you're sending the impression that you consider them as nothing more than a sounding board for your troubles.

Conclusion

If you're still wondering why others dislike you, look again at the above signs and habits of unlikable people. Being likable has nothing to do with being gorgeous or intelligent! All you have to do is respect other people's time and opinions. When spending time with someone, you must pay close attention. Being open-minded, sensitive, and understanding automatically makes you likable. When you become more conscious of how other people perceive your behavior, you pave the route toward being more likable.

Chapter 8:

5 Tips for A More Creative Brain

Nearly all great ideas follow a similar creative process, and this article explains how this process works. Understanding this is important because creative thinking is one of the most useful skills you can possess. Nearly every problem you face in work and life can benefit from creative solutions, lateral thinking, and innovative ideas.

Anyone can learn to be creative by using these five steps. That's not to say being creative is easy. Uncovering your creative genius requires courage and tons of practice. However, this five-step approach should help demystify the creative process and illuminate the path to more innovative thinking.

To explain how this process works, let me tell you a short story.

A Problem in Need of a Creative Solution

In the 1870s, newspapers, and printers faced a very specific and very costly problem. Photography was a new and exciting medium at the time. Readers wanted to see more pictures, but nobody could figure out how to print images quickly and cheaply.

For example, if a newspaper wanted to print an image in the 1870s, they had to commission an engraver to etch a copy of the photograph onto a steel plate by hand. These plates were used to press the image onto the page, but they often broke after a few uses. This process of photoengraving, you can imagine, was remarkably time-consuming and expensive.

The man who invented a solution to this problem was named Frederic Eugene Ives. He became a trailblazer in the field of photography and held over 70 patents by the end of his career. His story of creativity and innovation, which I will share now, is a useful case study for understanding the five key steps of the creative process.

A Flash of Insight

Ives got his start as a printer's apprentice in Ithaca, New York. After two years of learning the ins and outs of the printing process, he began managing the photographic laboratory at nearby Cornell University. He spent the rest of the decade experimenting with new photography techniques and learning about cameras, printers, and optics.

In 1881, Ives had a flash of insight regarding a better printing technique.

"While operating my photo stereotypes process in Ithaca, I studied the problem of the halftone process," Ives said. "I went to bed one night in a state of brain fog over the problem, and the instant I woke in the morning saw before me, apparently projected on the ceiling, the completely worked out process and equipment in operation."

Ives quickly translated his vision into reality and patented his printing approach in 1881. He spent the remainder of the decade improving upon it. By 1885, he had developed a simplified process that delivered even better results. As it came to be known, the Ives Process reduced the cost of printing images by 15x and remained the standard printing technique for the next 80 years.

Alright, now let's discuss what lessons we can learn from Ives about the creative process.

The 5 Stages of the Creative Process

In 1940, an advertising executive named James Webb Young published a short guide titled, A Technique for Producing Ideas. In this guide, he made a simple but profound statement about generating creative ideas.

According to Young, innovative ideas happen when you develop new combinations of old elements. In other words, creative thinking is not about generating something new from a blank slate but rather about taking what is already present and combining those bits and pieces in a way that has not been done previously.

Most importantly, generating new combinations hinges upon your ability to see the relationships between concepts. If you can form a new link between two old ideas, you have done something creative.

Young believed this process of creative connection always occurred in five steps.

1. **Gather new material.** At first, you learn. During this stage, you focus on 1) learning specific material directly related to your task and 2) learning general material by becoming fascinated with a wide range of concepts.

2. **Thoroughly work over the materials in your mind.** During this stage, you examine what you have learned by looking at the facts from different angles and experimenting with fitting various ideas together.

3. **Step away from the problem.** Next, you put the problem completely out of your mind and do something else that excites you and energizes you.

4. **Let your idea return to you.** At some point, but only after you stop thinking about it will your idea come back to you with a flash of insight and renewed energy.

5. **Shape and develop your idea based on feedback.** For any idea to succeed, you must release it out into the world, submit it to criticism, and adapt it as needed.

Chapter 9:
10 Habits of Emma Stone

Emma Stone, an Academy Award-winning actress made her debut in 2007 with the teen comedy "Superbad." Since then, she has become one of the most demanded actress of her time, amassing honours, nominations and captivating audiences on and off the big screen with her effortless, pleasant acting style and her attitude.

Stone's wide eyes and seemingly effortless brilliance shine through in practically every job she lands, making her one of the most renowned movies star. But, even if you've seen every one of Stone's films, there are likely a few facts you don't know about this extraordinary actress.

Here are 10 habits of Emma Stone that can be yours too.

1. Be Your Worst Judgement

According to Emma Stone, being your worst critique push you to work hard on yourself because your set standards are high. As long as you're true to yourself, what others think is not a concern. It's not about being cruel to oneself but about pushing yourself to new heights.

2. Understand Your Interests

Emma presented a PowerPoint presentation of her work to her parents for review. That earned her permission to relocate to Los Angeles in 2004 to pursue her acting career. She knew exactly what she wanted because it was her passion, and she didn't let anyone get in her way. You know you're enthusiastic about something when you're willing to go to any length to make it happen.

3. A Clear Vision

Stone is always quite clear about what she wants out of life. She does not allow short-term distractions or anything else to get in her way. She feels that the key to success is first to decide exactly what you want. The more precise your concept, the easier it will be to make it come to life.

4. Perseverance

Emma stone's route to Success, for example, her character Mia in La La La Land, was never an easy one. After she moved to California, she tried several roles, which was until 2007 she gained widespread notoriety for her appearance in the comedy "Superbad."
It took her five years have her first taste of success in acting. That kind of perseverance keeps her striving for the best, and so can you.

5. Education Equates No Worth

Stone has didn't allow societal assumptions and stigma to limit her. She made her acting debut when she was 11 years old. At the age of 15, she decided to drop out of high school and to pursue her acting career. In a world full of standardized tests, it is normal for people to assess you based on your educational level or even link it to your level of Success.

6. Eat that Dang Red Velvet Cupcake

The world is your oyster, and life is brief. So live your life, and don't allow anything to stop you from making the most of it.

7. No Barriers You Can't Conquer

Emma Stone revealed that she suffered from anxiety and panic attacks as a child. She opted for treatment and performance to help her get over it and keep chasing her aspirations. When you face challenges in your life, giving up is like giving up on the critical part of yourself. Losing faith in yourself means that your aspirations and passions are put on hold.

8. Do What Brings You Joy

If you are dissatisfied with your current circumstances, you must make a change. Life is too short to spend it doing things that make you miserable or even melancholy. For Emma, this means that you should treat yourself now and then, especially on bad days. Cherish the little things in life.

9. Look Up to Your Role Models

Emma broke down in tears when Mel B spoke to her through a video message. Of course, you don't have to cry when you meet your role model. But it's magnificent to have someone to look up to, that strong person who gives you strength on bad days.

10. Don't Over Plan

Having a precise aim and knowing where you want to go in life is absolutely a positive thing. But don't over plan because life might take an unexpected turn at any time. Emma, in an interview, said that she is a person who will never make a five-year plan and that she only depends on her intuition. Follow your intuition, and if it's correct, things will fall into place.

Conclusion

As Emma did, live your life, and don't allow anything to stop you from making the most of it.

Chapter 10:

8 Habits That Can Kill You

Toxic habits in our lives which when left unchecked can lead us to an early grave. We may not be aware of it but it is most definitely eating away at us slowly; like a frog gradually boiling to his death. These invisible yet harmful habits will start appearing in your life if you don't start taking note of it.

Here are 8 habits that can kill you if you're not careful:

1. Being a workaholic.

Man shall eat from the sweat of his brows. Our income pays our bills and puts food on the table. This infers that work is good for it is the backbone on which our survival is pegged upon. It is however not a license to bite more than you can chew. Drowning yourself at work is dangerous for your health.

There is a breaking point for every person. Workaholism is a habit that depressed people do to drown their misery. With only so much that you can handle, you will lose touch with the world if you work without a break. Workaholics are not hard workers who work to make ends meet. They are obsessed with work so that they can forget their problems.

If you are a workaholic who uses business to distract you from your problems, you run the risk of sinking to depression. Take note if stress disorders or suicidal thoughts start to appear. It may be time to seek help to deal with your problems head on instead of masking them in busyness.

2. Isolating yourself from others.

Withdrawal is a red flag any day, anytime. The moment you begin finding comfort in solitude, not wanting to associate with anyone, a problem is in the offing. However, there are times when you will need time alone to meditate and seek peace within yourself.

It is during withdrawal that suicidal thoughts are entertained and sometimes executed. When one isolates themselves from the rest of the world, he becomes blind and deaf to the reality on the ground. You seemingly live in a separate world often mistaken as one of tranquility and peace.

To fight isolation, always find a reason to be around people you share common interests with. It could be sports, writing, acting, or watching. This will help keep off loneliness.

3. Drug and substance abuse.

Drug abuse is a pitfall that many youths have fallen into. It will lead you to an early grave if you do not stop early enough. Apart from the long-term side effects on the health of addicts, drug abuse rips addicts off morality. Most of them become truants, finding themselves on the wrong side of the law and society.

Among the many reasons drug addicts give for drug abuse is that drugs give solace from the harsh world, some kind of temporary blissful haven which the soul longs for. It is unjustifiable to enter into such a health-damaging dungeon to contract respiratory diseases, liver disease, kidney damage, and cardiovascular diseases.

Be careful if you seek drugs as a way to escape from your troubles. If you look closely, most of these people do not end up in a good place after abusing these substances. Seek a healthier alternative instead to let off steam instead.

4. <u>Judging yourself by the standards of others.</u>

As Albert Einstein rightly put it; if we judge a fish by its ability to climb a tree, it will live its whole life believing it is stupid. It is erroneous to use other people's measurement of success to judge your own. This is not to say that you should not be appreciating the achievements of others, but as you do so, give yourself time and space for growth.

The pressure that comes with conforming to your peers' standards can push you down a dark path. Society can be so unforgiving for the faint-hearted. Once you are inside the dark hole of hopelessness, the air of gloom hangs over your head and it can lead you to an early grave. Everyone will forsake you when you fail even after trying to be like them.

5. <u>Being in the wrong company.</u>

Bad company ruins good morals. This truth is as old as civilization. It is not rocket science on how powerful the power of influence from friends is. When in the wrong company, you will be tagged into all sorts of activities they do. Isn't that a direct ticket to hades?

When you lose the power to say No and defend your integrity, morals, and everything that you believe in, then all hell will break loose on you. You would have handed your hypocrite friends the license to ruin your life. Not only will the wrong company ruin your life but also assassinate your character. Keep safe by fleeing from the wrong company when you can before it is too late.

6. <u>Lying.</u>

It looks simple but what many people do not consider is the effect of character assassination caused by a simple lie. Lying makes you unreliable. One client or employer will tell another one and before you know it no one wants anything to do with you.

It may not physically kill you but it will have the power to close all possible open doors of opportunities. Why not be genuine in your dealings and win the trust of your employers and clients? You should jealously protect your reputation because any assault at it is a direct attack on your integrity.

7. <u>Lack of physical exercise.</u>

A healthy body is a healthy mind. To increase your longevity, you need to have a healthy lifestyle. It is not always about the posh vehicle you are driving or the classy estate you live in. How physically fit you are plays a big role in determining your productivity.

You need to walk out there in the sun, go for a morning run, lift weights, do yoga and kegel exercises, or go swimming. Your body needs to be maintained by exercise and not dieting alone. It seems ignoble to be a field person but its benefits are immense.

8. <u>Poor nutritional habits.</u>

The risks of poor nutrition are uncountable. Overeating and obesity come from these habits. Few people pay attention to what they eat, ignorant of the consequences that follow.

Malnutrition and obesity are opposites but stemming from one source – poor nutrition. The eminent danger can no longer be ignored.

According to statistics from the World Health Organization, worldwide obesity has nearly tripled since 1975. In 2016 alone, more than 1.9 billion adults were overweight. The world health body acknowledges that the developmental, economic, social, and medical impacts of the global burden of malnutrition are serious and lasting, for individuals and their families, communities, and countries.

This has come as a shocker to us but it would not have been so if people paid attention to their nutrition habits.

All these 8 habits that can kill you are avoidable if caution is taken. The ball is in your court. Consider carefully whether you want to make a conscious decision to take responsibility and eliminate these damaging habits. You have the power to change if you believe in yourself.

PART 3

Chapter 1:

Do More of What Already Works

In 2004, nine hospitals in Michigan began implementing a new procedure in their intensive care units (I.C.U.). Almost overnight, healthcare professionals were stunned by its success.

Three months after it began, the procedure had cut the infection rate of I.C.U. Patients by sixty-six percent. Within 18 months, this one method had saved 75 million dollars in healthcare expenses. Best of all, this single intervention saved the lives of more than 1,500 people in just a year and a half. The strategy was immediately published in a blockbuster paper for the <u>New England Journal of Medicine</u>.

This medical miracle was also simpler than you could ever imagine. It was a checklist.

This five-step checklist was the simple solution that Michigan hospitals used to save 1,500 lives. Think about that for a moment. There were no technical innovations. There were no pharmaceutical discoveries or cutting-edge procedures. The physicians just stopped skipping steps. They implemented the answers they already had on a more consistent basis.

New Solutions vs. Old Solutions

We tend to undervalue answers that we have already discovered. We underutilize old solutions—even best practices—because they seem like something we have already considered.

Here's the problem: *"Everybody already knows that"* is very different from *"Everybody already does that."* Just because a solution is known doesn't mean it is utilized.

Even more critical, just because a solution is implemented occasionally doesn't mean it is implemented consistently. Every physician knew the five steps on Peter Pronovost's checklist, but very few did all five steps flawlessly each time.

We assume that new solutions are needed to make real progress, but that isn't always the case. This pattern is just as present in our personal lives as it is in corporations and governments. We waste the resources and ideas at our fingertips because they don't seem new and exciting.

There are many examples of behaviors, big and small, that have the opportunity to drive progress in our lives if we just did them with more consistency—flossing every day—never missing workouts. Performing fundamental business tasks each day, not just when you have time— apologizing more often. Writing Thank You notes each week.

Of course, these answers are boring. Mastering the fundamentals isn't sexy, but it works. No matter what task you are working on, a simple checklist of steps you can follow right now—fundamentals that you have known about for years—can immediately yield results if you just practice them more consistently.

Progress often hides behind boring solutions and underused insights. You don't need more information. You don't need a better strategy. You just need to do more of what already works.

Chapter 2:

5 Habits of Bill Gates

Bill gates is a name synonymous with success. Who does not know Bill Gates? His footprints are everywhere. Students in elementary school look up to him as their role model. Those in high school and higher levels of education idolize him. He is a semi-god, everyone wanting to identify himself or herself with his success.

Well, here are 5 habits of Bill Gates:

1. He Is Generous

The 65-year-old founder of Microsoft Corporation is by no means a mean person (pun intended). He has donated to charity drives uncountable times. Many students are beneficiaries of his generosity through the Bill & Melinda Gates Foundation. He has come out strongly to support the education of black and Latino students, and those experiencing poverty in the United States.

Bill Gates – co-chair and trustee of Bill & Melinda Gates Foundation – has committed over $1.75 billion over two years for Covid-19 pandemic relief. He, besides Mackenzie Scott, Warren Buffet, and George Soros are among the wealthiest most generous people.

He understands perfectly that to him who much is given, much will be expected. The world is full of praises for the generosity of the world's fourth-richest person. His foundation is the world's largest charitable foundation and he has not stopped at that. To the father of three, poverty eradication is one of his life-long goals.

We can take a cue from him and start giving to receive. We should not always be the recipients of charities. Learn to give, not out of abundance but out of the love for humanity.

2. He Treasures His Family

It is an open secret that the father of three is a family man. It is amazing how he has been able to keep his family together all those years despite his wealth. Until May 4th 2021, Bill was married to Melinda. In a statement sent to the BBC, they said it was regrettable that they had to end their 27-year-old marriage. Nevertheless, his contribution to keeping his family close to his chest cannot be ignored.

He has not allowed his family affairs to come out to the public. Even when he divorced his wife in May 2021, they issued a joint statement to the media and kept their divorce under wraps. This is unlike the noisy and messy divorces that most celebrities have.

We learn from Bill Gates the importance of family. It is always God first and family next. Treasure your family because blood is always thicker than water. Whenever there is conflict, do not let it spill out to the public but sort it out amicably.

3. He Is A Social Man

From public appearances in social functions to corporate events, Bill Gates does not shy away from the public. He takes his time to attend personally to matters that require his presence. He has learned not to build a fortress or isolate himself.

With the type of publicity he receives, a man of his stature would naturally want to lead a quiet life and focus primarily on his businesses. However, he has a strong online presence. Be it LinkedIn, Twitter, Instagram, or Facebook, he shares his thoughts fearlessly.

Moreover, the technology giant founder engages captains of industry in meaningful and fruitful conversations. He has embraced the human nature of socializing and talking to people. Likewise, we should follow in tow. We should not live in fortresses because we will be cut off from the outside world and that will be the beginning of our downfall.

Attend that lunch or dinner with your colleagues, go to the graduation party of your associates, attend birthday parties and weddings. It is these social events and more that will link you with potential destiny connectors and you will grow your network. Your network is your net worth.

4. He Is Conscious of His Public Image

Bill Gates has created for himself an image of a calm and composed leader. Dressed in smart elegant suits for every occasion, the multi-billionaire never fails to impress. Not once can you fault the man over his dress code. Have you ever heard of the saying "dress how you want to be addressed?"

Your dressing speaks volumes as to the kind of person you are. Dressing in itself is an art. Carefully observe not to underdress or overdress because it sends an unspoken message to those you meet.

Never has the 65-year-old billionaire been involved in a public saga. He is careful to carry himself with decorum whenever he is in public. Public perception is key to maintain his social stature – an art he has perfected over the years. Even the speech he gives is in tandem with his public image.

The thought that Bill Gates can speak rumors or even argue in public is unfathomable. He is a towering icon of success and is careful not to belittle his image. It takes a lifetime to build a reputation but a few minutes to ruin it completely.

5. He Has A Progressive Mindset

It all begins from the mind. Our mindset is what makes us stand out. It is easier for Bill Gates to be content with what he has achieved so far. He made history as the youngest American billionaire at 31 years until Zuckerberg broke that record in 2010.

He has received numerous accolades and awards for his work, but he is still not content at that level. This does not mean that Bill is ungrateful. He is grateful. It is only that he has set his mind on much higher targets. That is the progressive mindset all of us ought to emulate.

Most people fall into the trap of settling down for less in the name of being altruistic. It is time to stop getting comfortable and borrow a page from the lifestyle of Bill. The mind is where reason is born. Bill

Gates knows this perfectly well and despite his wealth and achievements, he keeps moving forward.

Bill's progressive mindset has made him grow his corporation to become the world's biggest company with a valuation of $1 trillion. It begins and ends with the mind.

The above are 5 habits of Bill Gates that he has developed over time. They have made him who he is today.

Chapter 3:

Six Steps To Create A Vision For Your Life

Hi everyone, for today's video, we are going to talk about how to create life's visions. You might be thinking, "why do we need to make these visions?" or "what are these visions for?".

Let me ask you this question, have you ever felt so stuck in where you are? That feeling when you wanna move and be somewhere else because you don't like where you are but you don't know where to go either? That is the worst feeling ever, right?

Creating a vision for your life will save you from being stuck and lost. These visions are the pictures you create about the life that you want to live.

Here are 6 Steps To Start Envisioning Your Future

Step number 1, identify what matters to you. Ask yourself, "what's really important to me?". Is it health? Career? Wealth? Relationships? Passion? Time? It could be a balance of all those things. What legacy would you want to leave in this world? Identifying what truly matters to you and what you really value gives you a destination of where you want to be. Having these in mind, all your plans and decisions will be centered towards your destination.

Next step is thinking ahead, but at the same time, also believing that it is already happening for you right now. Be specific in chasing what you want, don't just simply limit yourself to what you think is socially acceptable. If you limit your choices to what seems to be reasonable, you are disconnecting yourself from your true potentialDon't compromise.. Be as audacious as you want to be, it's your own life anyway! You have all the right to dream as big as you want. Talk as if your dreams are happening right now. When you have this big dream, you won't settle for less just because it is what's available at the moment.

Step number 3, assess and challenge your motives. Ask yourself, "is this the kind of life I wanna live because it is what the society is expecting from me?", "am I doing this because this is what everybody else is doing?" Knowing your real motive towards your visions will help you uncover what your heart really desires. You might even be surprised by what you'll discover within you when you remove all the layers that the world has planted in you.

Next step, be sure that your visions are aligned with a purpose. You don't need to know exactly what your life purpose is, unless you've already figured that out somehow. But your visions should be relevant to how you want your life to be. For example, if your goal is to maintain your mental well-being, your vision might be to live your life peacefully while focusing on the things that truly matter. Your vision should serve you the purpose into making your life as pleasing as you want it.

Step number 5 is to be accountable for your own visions. Don't tie your visions into someone else's hands. Your visions may involve direct impact to others but make sure that your visions are not dependent on other people. Why? Because people, just like the seasons, change. People come and go. The version of the people in your life right now is not how they will be for the rest of their lives. And so are you. Hold these visions in your own hands and make sure you execute it diligently and faithfully.

Last step is to make room for changes. You will grow as a person, that is a fact. You won't have the same exact priorities all through your life. And that's okay. Whatever you want to change into is valid. Your goals and dreams are all valid. Changes are inevitable so don't be afraid if you have to change what's working for you from time to time.

While you are in the process of making your life's visions, be as creative as you can. Although the world is not a wish-granting factory, remember that through your hard work and perseverance, nothing is really impossible. You have everything in you to achieve your goals and live through your visions. You just need to be clear about what you really want or where you wanna be.

Remember that our days in this world are limited. We won't be able to live our lives to the fullest if we are just merely existing or living by default. We are humans. And as humans, we have the power to lead the life we truly desire. Sometimes, we are just one decision away from it.

I hope what we've talked about today will not just inspire you to make your life's visions but also help you to understand why you need to make them. You deserve a kind of life that will excite you to wake up everyday because you know what you are waking up for.

That's all for today's video. Please don't forget to like and subscribe. I'll see you on the next one!

Chapter 4:

9 Habits To Wake Up Early

Waking up early is a real struggle for many people. People are battling this friendly monster silently. Friendly because the temptation to snooze the alarm or turn it off completely when it rings in the morning is irresistible. Almost everyone can attest to cursing under their breath when they hear their alarm go off loudly in the morning.

Here are 9 habits that you should strive to incorporate into your life if you wish to make waking early a part of your routine:

1. Sleeping early.

It is simple – early to bed, early to rise. Retiring to bed early will give you enough time to exhaust your sleep. The average person ought to have at least 8 hours of sleep. Sleeping early will create more time for rest and enable you to wake up on time.

Since sleep is not ignorable, you may be embarrassed when you find yourself sleeping when attending a meeting, or when you are at work. Save yourself this shame by sleeping early to wake up earlier.

After a long day of vicissitudes, gift your body the pleasure of having a good night's rest. Create extra time for this by lying horizontally early enough.

2. Scheduling your plans for the day beforehand.

A good plan is a job half done. Before the day ends, plan for the activities of the next day. When it is all mapped out, you will sleep with a clear mind on what you will be facing the next day. Planning is not a managerial routine task alone but everyone's duty of preparing to fight the unknown the following day.

Waking up early is a difficult decision to make impromptu because of the weakness in yielding to the temptation of 'sleeping for only five more minutes.' Having a plan gives you a reason to wake up early.

3. Creating deadlines.

Working under pressure is an alternative motivation for waking up early if planning has failed. With assignments to submit within a short time, or work reports to be submitted on short notice, the need to wake up early to beat these deadlines will be automatic.

We can create deadlines and ultimatums for ourselves without waiting on our superiors to impose them on us. This self-drive will last longer and it will increase our productivity instead of waiting for our clients and employers to give us ultimatums.

4. Being psychologically prepared.

The mind is the powerhouse of the body. Mental preparedness is the first step towards making and sticking to landmark decisions. The mind should initiate and accept the idea of waking up early before you can comfortably adopt this new routine.

Develop a positive attitude towards rising early and all other subsequent results will fall in place. The first person you need to convince to move towards a particular cause is you. As simple as waking up early seems, many people are grappling with late coming.

This is fixable by making a conscious decision to turn around your sleeping habits. The greatest battle is fought in the mind, where the body antagonizes the spirit.

5. Finding like-minded friends.

Birds of the same feathers flock together. When you are in the company of friends with one routine, your habits are fortified. With no dissenting voice amongst your friends to discourage you from waking up early, your morning routine will find a permanent spot in your life.

The contrary is true. When you are the odd one out in a clique of friends who have no regard for time, you are likely to lose even the little time-consciousness you had. They will contaminate you with their habits and before you know it, you will slip back to your old self (an over sleeper).

When you also decide to be a loner and not associate with those with the same habits as yourself, then you risk giving up on the way. The psych from friends will be lacking and soon you will just revert to your old habits.

When you want to walk fast, walk alone. When you want to go far, walk with others.

6. Being sensitive to your environment.

It takes a man of understanding to read and understand the prevailing times and seasons. You may occasionally visit a friend or a relative and spend the night. How can you wake up way past sunrise in a foreign environment? This will suggest to your hosts that you are lazy.

Create a good image by waking up a little bit early. If allowed, help do some morning chores over there.

Adjust your routine accordingly. Win over people by waking up early to join them in their morning chores. It is there where friendships are forged. A simple habit of waking up early can be an avenue to make alliances.

7. Addressing any health issues early.

In case of any underlying health conditions that can stop you from waking up early in the morning, seek medical help fast. You may be willing to be an early riser but may be suffering from asthma triggered by the chilly weather in the morning.

When that condition is controlled, you can also manage to wake up a little bit earlier than before and engage in health-friendly activities in the morning. It is a win-win. In either case, going for a medical check-up frequently will keep you healthy to wake up early.

Your health is a priority and when taken care of you will wake up early.

8. It is a habit for the successful.

Ironically, those who have made it in life wake up earlier than the less established ones. One would think that it is the place of the less-founded ones to rise early to go to work and do business so that they can be at par with the wealthy and mighty. Instead, the reverse is true.

Follow the footsteps of great leaders who wake up early to attend to their affairs. They have become who they are because they give no room to the laziness of waking up late. We all have 24 hours in a day to do our businesses, where does the gap between the haves and the have-nots come from? That gap comes from how we use our time.

9. Having a cheerful Spirit.

A cheerful spirit finds joy in even what seems trivial. You should not see waking up early as punishment. It should be a routine to be followed happily religiously. When you have a cheerful spirit, knowing for whose benefit you rise early, then it will be a habit engraved into your spirit.

The above 9 habits to wake up early are key to discovering our purpose and build a new routine henceforth of being an early riser. The most successful people in the world abide by this routine so why not make it yours too.

Chapter 5:

How To Focus on Creating Positive Actions

Only a positive person can lead a healthy life. Imagine waking up every day feeling like you are ready to face the day's challenges and you are filled with hope about life. That is something an optimist doesn't have to imagine because they already feel it every day. Also, scientifically, it is proven that optimistic people have a lower chance of dying because of a stress-caused disease. Although positive thinking will not magically vanish all your problems, it will make them seem more manageable and somewhat not a big deal.

Positive thinking is what leads to positive actions, actions that affect you and the people around you. When you think positively, your actions show how positive you are. You can create positive thinking by focusing on the good in life, even if it may feel tiny thing to feel happy about because when you once learn to be satisfied with minor things, you would think that you no longer feel the same amount of stress as before and now you would feel freer. This positive attitude will always find the good in everything, and life would seem much easier than before.

Being grateful for the things you have contributed a lot to your positive behavior. Gratitude has proven to reduce stress and improve self-esteem. Think of the things you are grateful for; for example, if someone gives you good advice, then be thankful to them, for if someone has helped you with something, then be grateful to them, by being grateful about minor things, you feel more optimistic about life, you feel that good things have always been coming to you. Studies show that making down a list of things you are grateful for during hard days helps you survive through the tough times.

A person laughing always looks like a happy person. Studies have shown that laughter lowers stress, anxiety, and depression. Open yourself up to humor, permit yourself to laugh even if forced because even a forced laugh can improve your mood. Laughter lightens the mood and makes problems seem more manageable. Your laughter is contagious, and it may even enhance the perspective of the people around us.

People with depression or anxiety are always their jailers; being harsh on themselves will only cause pain, negativity, and insecurity. So try to be soft with yourself, give yourself a positive talk regularly; it has proven to affect a person's actions. A positive word to yourself can influence your ability to regulate your feelings and thoughts. The positivity you carry in your brain is expressed through your actions, and who doesn't loves an optimistic person. Instead of blaming yourself, you can think differently, like "I will do better next time" or "I can fix this." Being optimistic about the complicated situation can lead your brain to find a solution to that problem.

When you wake up, it is good to do something positive in the morning, which mentally freshens you up. You can start the day by reading a positive quote about life and understand the meaning of that quote, and you may feel an overwhelming feeling after letting the meaning set. Everybody loves a good song, so start by listening to a piece of music that gives you positive vibes, that gives you hope, and motivation for the day. You can also share your positivity by being nice to someone or doing something nice for someone; you will find that you feel thrilled and positive by making someone else happy.

Surely you can't just start thinking positively in a night, but you can learn to approach things and people with a positive outlook with some practice.

Chapter 6:

9 Habits of Successful Students

Successful students are made up of a common DNA. This is because they share a backbone – their success. In the words of Aristotle, *we are what we repeatedly do. Excellence, then, is not an act, but a habit.* Success is a habit that this clique of students has perfected meticulously.

Here are 9 habits of successful students:

1. <u>They Identify With Their Status</u>

It begins at the beginning. It is a paradox in itself. The start of the success of successful students (pun intended) is their acceptance that they are students of whatever discipline they are pursuing. When they correctly identify with their discipline, the journey begins.

Next, they identify with the institution/person under whose tutelage they are placed. Appreciating the expertise of their seniors is as important as it is that they are successful. No one crowns himself King; Kingmakers do crown him or her. In this case, the institution provides the opportunity for the student and teacher to meet.

Successful students, at all levels, identify with their centers of learning. Be it primary school, high school, technical-vocational colleges, or universities, successful students are proud of them (at least during the duration of their study).

2. They Have A Good Attitude

How does the attitude of students connect with their success? Again, why are successful students proud of where they learn? If they have a bad attitude towards their centers of learning, they will dislike their teachers – those responsible for imparting knowledge to them. As a result, whatever they learn will not stick.

Successful students are as good as their attitude is towards their teachers, institutions, and discipline of study. If you want to master your studies then change your attitude. A good attitude opens you up to greater possibilities. The possibilities that will be open to you are infinite.

3. They Relate Well With Their Tutors

The relationship between learners and their teachers should strictly be professional (there is the risk of unethical behavior if it crosses that line). When learners are in harmony with their tutors, learning is easier.

A good relationship between students and teachers breeds trust. Trust is the foundation upon which success is founded. The goodwill of both the teacher and the student is based on the relationship between them. The former being devoted to the latter's needs and the latter submissive to the former's instructions.

Ask top candidates of national examinations how their relationship with their teachers was and you will hear of nothing short of "the best."

4. They Are Willing To Go The Extra Mile

The story of successful students is akin to a fairytale in a fairyland. The prince does everything to protect his bride. He will go the extra mile to make her happy, to know her better, and even to cheer her up. With this infinite love, either of them is ready to move mountains for the sake of the other.

Successful students and their studies are like the groom and bride in the fairyland. The students do not mind going an extra mile for their bride (studies). They study late into the night, sacrifice their free time to grasp new concepts, and are even ready to forego short-time pleasures for the sake of their education.

This sacrifice is what distinguishes them from the rest of their peers.

5. <u>They Are Inquisitive</u>

Successful students are always curious about what they do not know. The unknown stirs curiosity in them; they are never content with the status quo. Their inquisitive nature is gold – a rare characteristic in most students. A majority of them are satisfied with what they know.

Their inquisitiveness births innovation. While settling for nothing short of the best, they try out new practices, re-design existing models and create new inventions. They stand out from their peers. Being inquisitive is not disrespect for authority or existing knowledge. On the contrary, it is appreciating the current principles and building on them to come up with something better.

6. <u>They Have Focus</u>

Their primary goal is clear and everything else is secondary. Successful students have a razor-sharp focus of the eagle, not distracted by anything that crosses their line.

A perfect real-life example is that of a hunting lion. When it settles on its prey from a herd, it chases it to the end. It can even pass other animals while chasing the specific target. The lion does not care whether the animal that crosses its path is better than its target. The only thing that matters is getting to its target.

When students decide to prioritize their education above any other interest, their energy and concentration are drawn to it. Success will be their cup of tea.

7. <u>They Do Their Due Dilligence</u>

The art of assuming is foreign to successful students. They treat everything in their discipline with utmost care. They research on results of experiments and answer the whys that arise.

It is never said by their tutors that they neglected their duty of research. Successful students know their role and they play it well. They know where and when to stop. This makes them disciplined compared to their colleagues.

Their discipline is outstanding. Shape your discipline and you will join the exclusive club of successful students.

8. <u>Abide By The Book</u>

Successful students stick to the rules of the game. This is important since it is not all students who manage to complete the race. Like any other commitment, learning requires agility. It has its own rules, the common and the silent rules. Most important are the unspoken rules that students are expected to abide by.

What is left unsaid, for example, is that students are not expected to be in romantic relationships because it will get in the way of their education.

9. They Are Punctual

Successful students keep time. Punctuality is the backbone of planning which is very important for focused people. Keeping time helps students avoid missing classes and group discussions or arriving very late for the same.

Success itself arrives punctually in the sense that it gives proportionate results to the input invested by those who court it. Successful students are the best timekeepers. Those who do not observe time have learned the hard way how to.

These 9 habits are what successful students do to make it to the top and stay there.

Chapter 7:

How to Build Skills That Are Valuable

The most valuable skills you can have in life and work are rarely taught in school, never show up on a resume, and are consistently overlooked and underappreciated. But there's some good news: It costs nothing to develop them, and you have the opportunity to do so.

Here's how

1. The Ability To Pay Attention

The shorter the average attention span gets, the more valuable your ability to focus becomes.

It's a huge competitive advantage to be able to pay attention to things for an extended period (and unfortunately, what passes for an extended period these days may be as little as 10 minutes).

The ability to pay attention helps you learn, communicate, be productive, and see opportunities others miss, among countless other things.

Two ways to improve your ability to pay attention:

- Practice single-tasking — read a book, watch a movie, or find some other thing to do for an extensive amount of time without allowing yourself to do anything else during that time. No side conversations. No checking your phone. Nothing but focus on that one thing.

- Become intentional with how you use your phone (and for the love of God, turn off your notifications!).

2. The Ability To Follow Directions

This one takes your improved ability to pay attention a step further.

Every aspect of your life and career involves directions —customers tell you what they want, your boss tells you what she needs to be done, and the people you care about tell you what they expect of you.

It's one thing to pay attention to instructions, but it's another to accurately follow them.

The best qualifications in the world won't land you a job if your application doesn't include the employer's requested details.

Your company won't care about your innovative ideas if they don't align with the problems they asked you to solve.

And the reason Facebook Ads may not work for you isn't that Facebook ads don't work — it's because you don't know the right ways to use them.

The ability to follow directions serves as a filter that keeps otherwise qualified people from succeeding — and most of them don't even realize their struggles are rooted in this weakness.

Don't let that be you.

Two ways to improve your ability to follow directions:

1. Ask for directions on how to do things more often. Practice makes perfect.

2. Give directions to other people. Take something you know how to do (like write a blog post, for example), and write up directions to help others do it the way you do (like I did here). Teaching is a great way to learn, and the process of creating directions will help you recognize the importance of little steps in directions you get from others.

The point of this post isn't to make you feel overwhelmed. The truth is, you already have these skills — we all do. But I wrote this because I've noticed many people don't think about these abilities as skills and therefore don't do much to hone them.

Chapter 8:

10 Habits of Lady Gaga

Stefani Joanne Angelina Germanotta, the one-and-only Lady Gaga is known for her unique approach to music and life. The iconic American singer, songwriter, and actress has captivated audiences with her talent and kindness, her creative stage appearances, and her dedicated support of the LGBT community and anti-bullying campaigns.

Like many other great success stories, her path to fame was fraught with hiccups, including dropping out of school, being dropped by Def Jam, and eventually writing for Sony. This encounter introduced her to Akon, who assisted her in signing a deal and releasing her first album. Her career has yielded several Guinness World Records, twelve Grammy awards, an Oscar, a BAFTA award, two Golden Globes, and numerous other honors.

Here are 10 Habits of Lady Gaga.

1. She's Inspired by What's Next

Focusing on the present and future makes you the happiest and successful person. During an interview with Oprah, Gaga shared, "I know it's there, but can I open it?" It's not only writing one song; it's also writing the next. It's writing the next chapter of whichever lobe in my brain is still locked."

2. Lady Gaga Owns Fame

Faking it till you make it is a part of almost everyone's game for attention and legacy building. Although it may necessitate a bit of bravado, it puts in a happy outlook and a great groove. If you don't like this phrase, consider Gaga's fine art of manifestation, she saw herself as a success story which eventually laid a ground for her career.

3. Be unique

Lady Gaga is unmistakable in her uniqueness. She distinguishes herself from many female pop artists by her physical appearances, acting, performances, song-writing, and her unique electric genre. You have to be one-of-a-kind, unusual, and shine in your way.

4. Create an Experience To Tell Your Story

Lady Gaga knows how to create a game-changing experience that truly embodies who she is and what she wants to communicate. Think of 2011 Grammy Awards when she was carried down the red carpet in an egg by staffers dressed in a suggestive egg-shell lie outfit? Whatever you are communicating will be memorable, when you relay it through experiences.

5. Don't Conform to Others' Opinions

Everyone will have an opinion on everything, and if you let them, they may influence how you see yourself. Or how you go about your daily existence. For Gaga, getting advice is not something she takes lightly; instead, she vets whoever offers it. "Only respect those whose opinions you appreciate." she told CNN.

6. Reinvent When Something Isn't Working

Find new ways to getting things done when it's not working anymore. Lady Gaga has dabbled in acting gigs (American Horror Story and A Star Is Born), all while expanding her fan base and showing her diverse talents.

7. Her Art Is Her Solace

During an interview with Rolling Stone, Gaga compared her music with addiction to heroin, suggesting that music is her solace. When you love what you do, no matter the industry, you commit yourself to the struggle and pain that comes with it. It is through ups and downs that you can appreciate your process.

8. Creativity and Hard Work Fuel Her Day-And Her Life

Although singing and writing are natural talents, Gaga is quick to warn aspiring musicians and performers that hard work and sacrifice counts. Gaga believes that learning and mastering your craft should let the you shine through, regardless of the critics. She understands that grit will be the secret ingredient that gets you there.

9. Lead With Values

Gaga constantly advocates for people in society who are ostracized and bullied because they are different such as LGBT. When you identify yourself with beliefs or things that connect with other people, you'll definitely earn their loyalty.

10. She Stays True to Her Personality

Being a leader in your craft entails keeping true to yourself rather than being a follower. If you work as a janitor, be a visionary janitor who instills wonder in your work. Lady Gaga does not behave in a way that is meant to please the public. She forges her way through her outlandish clothes and great performances. Then there's the lead.

Conclusion

It doesn't matter if you have fans, customers, clients, employees, or Gaga's "little monsters." This is how it works, even if you weren't born with the same genes as Lady Gaga. When we push the envelope and step outside of your comfort zone, amazing things happen. Rock your way through!

Chapter 9:

10 Habits of Ariana Grande

You may remember Ariana Grande from her early days as Cat Valentine on the Nickelodeon sitcoms "Victorious" and her show "Sam and Cat," as well as her music, including her latest album, "Positions." Her career took off after she decided to pursue music. She creates music that combines pop, Electronica, and R&b music.

Ariana Grande is an American singer and actress with over 126 awards in her music career. She is also an activist who has constantly been speaking out in support of women and LGBT rights. Her superpowers, both on and off stage, have landed her on time's list of the world's most influential people.

Although she is well known for her powerful vocals, there is way lot more to her than you know. Here are 10 Ariana Grande habits that might intrigue you.

1. She Puts Her Ego Aside

It's easy to let your ego kick in when the world is constantly talking about you. But for Ariana Grande, her ego and what she loves doing can't mingle as it can drag her work, which she finds unacceptable.

When does your ego get in the way of your masterpiece? Are you spending more time focusing on other people's work or on what other people have to say? Take a cue from Ariana Grande.

2. She Stands Her Ground

As a feminist, Ariana does not let anyone or anything get in her way, but she does so professionally. Possibly Grande explains it best when she encourages others to be themselves rather than living up to expectations. You can be gorgeous and clever, nice and goofy while strong and invincible as well as simultaneously sexual and entertaining.

3. She Maintains a Healthy Environment

Ariana Grande has held fast to her roots by surrounding herself with health and love. Her circle of friends and family are people she grew up with within Boca Raton. Keeping close to people that matter more in her life help her stay grounded and sane.

Your surrounding will influence your habits and behaviour towards improving and moving quickly.

4. She Does Her Own Thing

There are certain steps that everyone has taken when advancing through the ranks of whichever industry they chose. Like you start here and work your way up, doing this first, then that.

Just because there is a historical record of how things were doesn't mean they have to stay that way. Grande is a beautiful example of this: her dream was to be a singer, but she wanted to release songs in the way that a rapper does.

5. Continues Improving

Do you have a plan to improve? It would be ideal if you monitored your habits daily to ensure that you are consistently showing up and making modest improvements to your life. Ariana Grande surpassed her heavy net worth by improving and staying on top of her game. From "victorious" to creating her show "Sam and Cat" to building an empire through her music career.

6. She Takes Care of Her Emotional Wellbeing

If Grande's hit song "thank u, next" doesn't express her dating review, consider this: she guards her mental space. She constantly reminds her fans how important it is to protect their mental health and peace. Ground, exhaust, and conserve your mental health with the right energy.

7. She Makes Her Dreams Come True

Just like Ariana, manifest it! Ask any new life guru, astrology, or life coach, and they'll insist on manifestation. This is the where you envision, believe and trust that the things you desire will fall into place.

8. Simplicity Is Her Fineness

Looking like Ariana Grande may be your dream and a challenge too. When it comes to self-care, simplicity characterizes her. Ariana maintains a vegan diet, takes regular strolls, and naps enough to keep her health intact.

9. Don't Let Haters Get Your Cool

Ariana got blamed for her Ex-boyfriend, Mac Miller death, and aftermath of Manchester bombing. Despite these, she managed to ace her record-breaking album "sweeter" to honour the lives lost during the bombing.

10. Looks Don't Define You

Occasionally, Ariana reminds her fans not to allow their looks or weight define who they really are. No one is perfect, just be true to your sweet self.

Conclusion

Ariana is a true sweetheart, and above all, she seems to be growing much stronger despite all the backlash she receives publicly. Even though you don't agree with all her actions, there is definitely something to grasps from her habits.

Chapter 10:

8 Ways To Gain Self-Confidence

Confidence is not something that can be inherited or learned but is rather a state of mind. Confidence is an attribute that most people would kill to possess. It comes from the feelings of well-being, acceptance of your body and mind (your self-esteem), and belief in your ability, skills, and experience. Positive thinking, knowledge, training, and talking to other people are valuable ways to help improve or boost your confidence levels. Although the definition of self-confidence is different for everyone, the simplest one can be 'to have faith and believe in yourself.'

Here are 8 Ways To Gain More Self-Confidence:

1. Look at what you have already achieved:

It's easy to lose confidence when we dwell on our past mistakes and believe that we haven't actually achieved anything yet. It's common to degrade ourselves and not see our achievements as something special. But we should be proud of ourselves even if we do just a single task throughout the day that benefited us or the society in any way. Please make a list of all the things you are proud of, and it can be as small as cleaning your room or as big as getting a good grade or excelling in your job. Keep adding your small or significant achievements every day. Whenever you feel low in confidence, pull out the list and remind yourself how far you have come, how many amazing things you have done, and how far you still have to go.

2. Polish the things you're already good at:

We feel confident in the things we know we are good at. Everyone has some kind of strengths, talents, and skills. You just have to recognize what's yours and work towards it to polish it. Some people are naturally good at everything they do. But that doesn't make you any less unique. You have to try to build on those things that you are good at, and they will help you built confidence in your abilities.

3. Set goals for yourself daily:

Whether it's cooking for yourself, reading a book, studying for a test, planning to meet a friend, or doing anything job-related, make a to-do list for yourself daily. Plan the steps that you have to take to achieve them. They don't necessarily have to be big goals; you should always aim for small achievements. At the end of the day, tick off all the things you did. This will help you gain confidence in your ability to get things done and give you a sense of self-appreciation and self-worth.

4. Talk yourself up:

That tiny voice inside of our heads is the key player in the game of our lives. You'll always be running low on confidence if that voice constantly has negative commentary in your mind telling you that you're not good enough. You should sit somewhere calm and quiet and talk to yourself out of all the negative things. Treat yourself like you would treat a loved one when they tend to feel down. Convince yourself that you can achieve anything, and there's nothing that can stop you. Fill your mind with positive thoughts and act on them.

5. Get a hobby:

Find yourself something that really interests you. It can either be photography, baking, writing, reading, anything at all. When you have found yourself something you are passionate about, commit yourself to it and give it a go. Chances are, you will get motivated and build skills more quickly; this will help you gain self-confidence as you would gradually get better at it and feel accomplished. The praises you will get for it will also boost your confidence.

6. Face your fears:

The best way to gain confidence is to face your fears head-on. There's no time to apply for a promotion or ask someone out on a date until you feel confident enough. Practice facing your fears even if it means that you will embarrass yourself or mess up. Remind yourself that it's just an experiment. You might learn that making mistakes or being anxious isn't half as bad as you would have thought. It will help you gain confidence each time you move forward, and it will prevent you from taking any risks that will result in negative consequences.

7. Surround yourself with positive people:

Observe your friends and the people around you. Do they lift you and accept who you are or bring you down and point out your flaws? A man is known by the company he keeps. Your friends should always positively influence your thoughts and attitude and make you feel better about yourself.

8. Learn To Strike A Balance:

Self-confidence is not a static measure. Some days, we might feel more confident than others. We might often feel a lack of confidence due to criticism, failures, lack of knowledge, or low self-esteem. While another time we might feel over-confident. We might come off as arrogant and self-centred to other people, and it can eventually lead to our failure. We should keep a suitable amount of confidence within ourselves.

Conclusion:

Confidence is primarily the result of how we have been taught and brought up. We usually learn from others how to behave and what to think of ourselves. Confidence is also a result of our experiences and how we learn to react in different situations. Everyone struggles with confidence issues at one time or another, but these quick fixes should enough to boost your confidence. Start with the easier targets, and then work yourself up. I believe in you. Always!

CPSIA information can be obtained
at www.ICGtesting.com
Printed in the USA
BVHW042257051221
623306BV00017B/670

9 781913 710972